The Route Map to Business Continuity Management

Management

Meeting the Requirements of ISO 22301

The Route Map to Business Continuity Management

Meeting the Requirements of ISO 22301

John Sharp

First published in the UK in 2008

by

BSI Standards Limited

389 Chiswick High Road

London W4 4AL

Second edition published in 2012

Typeset in Great Britain by Letterpart Limited, letterpart.com

Printed in Great Britain by Berforts Group, www.berforts.co.uk

British Library Cataloguing in Publication Data

A catalogue record for this book is available from the British Library

ISBN 978 0 580 74341 2

Contents

Preface

This book has been written to help those managers who have decided, or who have been tasked, to introduce business continuity management (BCM) into their organization. It is based on the new international standard for BCM – ISO 22301:2012 and on the Plan-Do-Check-Act model used by the new standard and other management systems, such as BS EN ISO 9001, *Quality management systems* and BS EN ISO 14001, *Environmental management systems*. The British Standard for BCM, BS 25999 Parts 1 and 2, on which the first edition of this book was based, was used extensively in the creation of ISO 22301.

The book includes brief case studies to illustrate the main ideas of BCM, and templates to assist with the various stages of the BCM process.

Those seeking to implement BCM are encouraged to build on what already exists in their organization, e.g. IT disaster recovery plans, risk management, security and safety management and personnel succession planning. They are further encouraged to involve representatives from all departments and support functions to achieve a uniform approach to BCM and a more resilient organization.

Chapter 1   Introduction

Business continuity management (BCM) is a management discipline that has become increasingly important given the turbulent environments in which organizations now find themselves.

There are three types of risks that organizations now face: known risks such as utility failures or fires, which can be identified, quantified and planned for; emerging risks such as animal or human flu pandemics whose impact cannot be fully determined; and unforeseen risks that can have a major impact. In 2007, the author Nassim Nicholas Taleb put forward the concept of 'black swans' to describe unforeseen events that hit organizations without warning: an example is the 2011 Japanese earthquake, tsunami and subsequent nuclear accident.

When these risks materialize they can cause major disruption to communities and organizations, resulting in the failure to deliver products and services that support the economic life and welfare of communities as a whole.

It is not just major events that can cause a break in continuity of operations. One in five UK organizations suffers a disruptive event every year caused by lower-level incidents such as sickness, loss of technology, denial of access to its site or loss of a key supplier. These events may not impact on the wider community but could lead to the failure of an individual organization through disruption to cash flow or loss of confidence and reputation by its customers and clients. By adopting BCM, organizations will be better equipped to meet the challenges they face when disrupted, whatever the reason, thus protecting themselves and the wider community they serve.

In 2003 the British Standards Institution (BSI) published a Publicly Available Specification, PAS 56, *Guide to business continuity management*, which drew together the best practice in BCM and was adopted by many organizations throughout the world.

In 2006 PAS 56 was withdrawn and replaced by a new British Standard for BCM: BS 25999-1, providing a code of practice for BCM. The document incorporated the best practice from PAS 56, the BCM guidelines that support the UK Civil Contingencies Act 2004 and other sources from around the world. In 2007 BSI published BS 25999-2 that provided a Specification against which organizations could seek certification.

In 2007 the United Kingdom Accreditation Service (UKAS) launched an accreditation scheme for certification bodies and by 2012 eight companies had been accredited by UKAS to issue certification against BS 25999-2. During this period many organizations across the world have achieved certification.

In 2012 the International Organization for Standardization (ISO) issued a new standard, ISO 22301, that provides new requirements/specifications for BCM. This standard is to be complemented by new BCM guidance – ISO 22313.

The first edition of this book was written to assist those organizations wishing to comply with the British Standard BS 25999-2. This edition is designed to help organizations meet the requirements in the new standard for BCM, ISO 22301, and builds upon the work that many organizations have already undertaken to gain certification or align their BCM to BS 25999-2.

Evolution of BCM

The concept of business continuity was developed in the mid-1980s as a new way of managing business risks. The basis of BCM is that it is the key responsibility of company directors to ensure the continuation of business functionality at all times and under any circumstances.

BCM grew out of requirements in the early 1970s to provide computer disaster recovery for information systems. Traditionally disaster planning had concentrated on the restoration of facilities after a major incident, such as the loss of computing or telecommunications, or the loss of a building or plant through fire or flood. The responsibility for these plans had been dispersed to various functions within a company. Typically these were the IT, estates and security departments. Disaster recovery plans in general are written on the basis of recovery after a disruptive incident.

Unexpected events do not simply happen; quite often they are created by the organization itself. Every organization has inherent weaknesses: faulty IT systems that are 'worked around', informal communication channels, lack of operator training, disconnects in structures and local procedure variations. Examination into the causes of most major disasters has found that there are several incidents or circumstances that combine together, leading to the eventual disaster.

BCM is about prevention, not just cure. It is not just about being able to deal with incidents as and when they occur and thus prevent a crisis and subsequent disaster, but also about establishing a culture within the organization that seeks to build in greater resilience in order to ensure the continuity of operations to deliver key products and/or services to clients and customers.

BCM establishes a strategic and operational framework to implement, proactively, an organization's resilience to disruption. It is not purely a reactive measure taken after an incident has occurred. BCM requires planning across many facets of an organization. Its resilience depends equally on its management and operational staff, as well as technology and facilities. It is essential to take a holistic approach when establishing a BCM programme.

BCM is about anticipating that things are about to go wrong and taking planned and rehearsed steps to protect the business and hence the needs and expectations of interested parties. It is about maintaining their confidence in the management's ability to handle a crisis and to prevent disasters occurring, thus protecting the brand, reputation and image of the organization as much as its physical infrastructure and employees. BCM goes beyond recovery from a disaster to establishing a culture that seeks to prevent failure and crisis.

Knight and Pretty of Templeton College, Oxford, undertook research in the mid-1990s that showed that the impact of disasters on shareholder value could be serious (Knight and Pretty, 2000). They discovered that it is the lack of confidence in the ability of senior managers and directors to act quickly and professionally at the time of disaster that drives down share values. This was further backed up by the Cass Business School study into major risk events, *Roads to Ruin*, published in 2011 by Airmic. The study investigated 18 high-profile corporate crises of the past decade. Most of the companies – and their shareholders – suffered severe, uninsurable losses and most reputations suffered severe damage. None of the companies emerged without obvious immediate harm. Among the seven issues identified were inadequate board skills to exercise control, blindness to inherent risks, such as risks to the business model or reputation, inadequate leadership on ethos and culture, defective internal communication and information flow, and organizational complexity and change.

> The BP Gulf of Mexico disaster of 2010 is a classic example of what can go wrong when the senior management mishandles a crisis. The share price fell 54 per cent in three months and two years later was still 23 per cent below the price prior to the disaster. The CEO lost his job, the company was forced to sell off many of its assets to set aside funds to cover claims that in 2011 exceeded £35 billion. In addition a lucrative deal with the Russians was lost to another international oil company.

Effective BCM integrates with crisis/incident management to ensure that if a major incident does occur then not only is the organization able to maintain continuity of operations, it is also able to reassure the interested parties that it is in control.

The business drivers

Although it is widely accepted that the protection of brand, reputation and image is paramount for any organization, other, external, drivers may have greater influence over the introduction of BCM (see Figure 1).

Industry regulations and legal requirements are driving organizations to establish BCM. There is greater awareness among regulators that organizations should have effective BCM in place for the protection of customers and the community. Since the attack on the World Trade Centre in New York on 11 September 2001 and the global financial crisis of 2008 finance regulators across the world have set out conditions for BCM that they expect the firms they regulate to follow. In some cases these conditions are mandatory; in others they provide strong guidance.

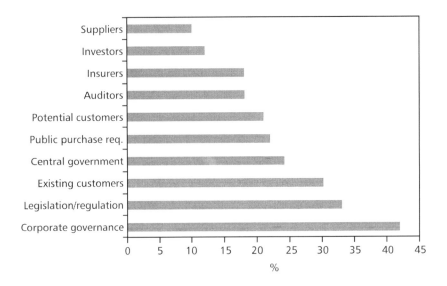

Figure 1 – External drivers for BCM

Source: Chartered Management Institute, 2012

In the UK the Civil Contingencies Act 2004 requires local government bodies, the National Health Service (NHS) and emergency services to put in place effective BCM to ensure that they can continue to perform their functions in the event of an emergency. They have to ensure they can mobilize the functions they need to deal with the emergency, minimize the impact on the responder's day-to-day activity, and maintain vital services for the community at an appropriate level. In addition local authorities have the responsibility of promoting business continuity to business and appropriate voluntary bodies in support of the concept of a resilient community.

Insurance companies are having an increasing influence. Business interruption insurance is seen as a way of covering the revenue lost following a major disruption. Until relatively recently the insurance market linked business interruption insurance to building insurance. They now seek to sever this link as business interruption losses have increased dramatically. Underwriters are looking for evidence that effective BCM is in place to reduce their risk exposure to business interruption.

One of the most significant drivers today is that of corporate governance. Across the world, regulation and legislation in this area is increasing. In the UK the revision of stock exchange listing rules places greater emphasis on internal controls to manage the principal risks facing a company.

When the Turnbull Committee's *Guidance for Directors* on internal controls was first published in September 1999 (Turnbull et al., 1999) the chair of the committee, Nigel Turnbull, stated, 'The Guidance sets out an overall framework of best practice for business, based upon an assessment and control of their significant risks. For many companies, business continuity management will address some of these key risks and help them to achieve compliance' (Nigel Turnbull, personal communication).

Auditors are acting as key external drivers as they look for evidence of effective BCM being in place to meet regulations and legislation. Previously they asked if business continuity plans (BCPs) existed. Their current approach is to look for evidence that the plan is rehearsed and that BCM has been promoted within the organization.

In the UK public authorities and emergency services that are driven by the Civil Contingencies Act are now the biggest drivers of BCM down the supply chain. Increasingly they are seeking evidence that their partners and suppliers have effective BCM; in many cases suppliers cannot tender unless they have implemented business continuity.

A local authority in the North West of England uses voluntary organizations to provide vital services, on the authority's behalf, to some of the most vulnerable in its community. It needs to be certain that these organizations are able to continue, especially at the time of a major emergency affecting the area.

The council department responsible for these services now requires that any organization receiving funding from the authority must have business continuity. The council offers help and advice to the voluntary organizations on the establishment of BCM.

Motivated by these external drivers and the need to manage principal risks, organizations have identified that they are often dependent upon key suppliers for their own continuity. As a result the pressure for BCM has started to flow down the supply chain from customers. Just as major customers have insisted that their suppliers have quality and project management processes in place, they are now also demanding that BCM be established to ensure continuity of supply. This is driven not only by their need to achieve regulatory compliance, but also by the need to maintain their market share. The Japanese earthquake/tsunami/nuclear accident, the volcanic ash cloud in 2011 and the increase in severe winter weather has highlighted the need for better continuity management across the supply network.

There are a number of factors that have emerged in recent decades that might be considered to have increased the level of risk in supply chains. These include: the adoption of 'lean' practices, the globalization of supply, focused factories and centralized distribution, the trend to outsourcing, reduction in the supplier base, volatility of demand and the lack of visibility and control procedures.

A breakdown of drivers by sector and organizational type is contained in Appendix A.

Future drivers may include investors and banks that would wish to see that continuity is built into business plans. Additional pressure may come from trade and professional bodies and the public in general via the media and pressure groups.

Time has become a key driver for BCM. The speed of business has changed and there is very often little time to allow for a gradual recovery. The emergence of e-commerce and the lack of loyalty among customers change the need for recovery to one of availability. Organizations for which this is vital have to ensure that their services are available 24 hours a day, seven days a week, 365 days a year. Customers will not wait if a call centre is not answering or a website is not available to place an order; they will go elsewhere. Failures can be the result of technical problems, high demand when a site opens for the first time or, more seriously, denial of service attacks by malicious individuals or organizations.

> Tickets for the 2012 Olympics in London were sold in various tranches over the internet. The demand for tickets was so great that when the official website opened it was swamped and crashed on several occasions. The media had extensive coverage of the failures and of applicants' disappointment.

Benefits of BCM

Implementing BCM can bring real benefits to an organization aside from meeting the regulatory and legal requirements.

Competitive advantage can be gained for organizations that are able to demonstrate to potential customers that they have proven plans to continue supply in the face of disruption. Certification against or compliance with ISO 22301 (and BS 25999-2 until transition to the new standard is achieved) can be used as part of a marketing package to attract new customers as well as providing existing customers with a positive reason to renew contracts.

Financial benefits will occur when areas of weakness within the organization are eliminated. Within processes, duplications and omissions exist that are wasteful in time and resources. Every failure that occurs has a cost to the organization, even if it does not result in a disruption. By eliminating these weaknesses the organization becomes more resilient and more cost-effective.

Further financial gain may occur if effective BCM exists as it can influence the approach taken by insurers to business interruption insurance. It can affect the level of cover offered, the amount of excess that is applied to a policy or reduce the premiums levied. More than 80 per cent of insurance brokers state that premium discounts are given if business continuity plans are in place (British Insurance Brokers' Association and UK Cabinet Office, 2012).

One of the greatest threats to an organization during a disruption is the interruption to cash flow. In enabling the continued delivery of key products and services, effective BCM contributes to the maintenance of cash flow. Following the global financial crisis, for many organizations this can be critical as they are dependent on their ability to maintain operations in order to service debt.

A printer ran a successful one-man business in a small UK town. He was reasonably priced and relatively quick. Five weeks before Christmas he had a problem with his press and could not print orders. He did not inform his customers of the difficulties but waited for them to contact him. He had no maintenance contract on his press and when he did get an engineer to the site he was advised that it was a machine for which there were no spares in stock and they would have to come from Japan.

It was three weeks before he was back in production. Many of his customers had gone elsewhere as they needed their printing completed before Christmas. As he was based in a small town his failing was soon known and his reputation suffered as a result. The following March he wrote to all his existing customers advising them that he was no longer able to continue to service their needs as the company was closing due to lack of business.

Key lessons for small companies:

- If you have a single machine on which you rely, ensure you have a maintenance contract in place with a company that services that model.
- Make arrangements with a similar company outside the area whereby you both undertake to meet the other company's orders in the event of being disrupted – mutual aid.
- And finally, if you have a problem, advise your customers and explain what you are doing to meet their requirements.

If correctly introduced, BCM encourages greater staff involvement in the successful running of the organization. By listening to the people who actually do the job it is possible to eliminate many of the lower-level risks that can disrupt an organization. It is often the front-line staff that can identify where weaknesses and single points of failure exist and how to improve processes and resilience. These staff will welcome an opportunity to contribute and have a chance for their ideas and concerns to be acknowledged and, if appropriate, implemented.

Every organization has a duty of care to its employees, customers, clients, the community and the environment as part of societal security. BCM can be seen as part of a social responsibility agenda, helping to discharge these duties and maintaining employment throughout the period of disruption.

The most valuable asset of any organization – public, private or voluntary – is its reputation; it can take years to build up and moments to destroy. Elements of BCM are designed to ensure that every effort is made to protect brand reputation and image throughout and beyond a period of disruption.

Chapter 2   Why adopt a business continuity standard?

As BCM has developed worldwide, there has been a convergence in the methodologies being promoted. It became apparent following the Year 2000 problem or 'millennium bug', when organizations were deluged with requests for compliance statements from their customers and clients, that there was a need for a uniform approach to BCM.

It is undesirable for major customers to enforce their own approach to BCM down their supply chains, as happened with other management systems, notably quality. While a supplier can run different quality systems to meet the requirements of its customer base, it cannot run different, and possibly conflicting, BCM systems, which will be used during a disruption at a time when tensions are high. This was one of the principal drivers for establishing BCM standards in the UK.

BS 25999 was created to set out a uniform benchmark in good practice, satisfying the needs of customers, clients, government, regulators and all other interested parties. BS 25999 has been accepted worldwide and has formed the basis of many other BCM standards, including the US ASIS/BSI BCM.01 standard adopted by ANSI. BS 25999 and other BCM standards from across the globe provided the source material for the creation of two new international standards: ISO 22301 (requirements) and ISO 22313 (guidance).

By adopting the standard approach to BCM as set out in ISO 22301, organizations can offer their customers and clients greater assurance that they will be capable of maintaining continuity of operations if they suffer disruptive incidents.

For those already certified to BS 25999-2 there will be a transition period to allow them to update the BCM systems to ISO 22301. For those certified, and those organizations working towards certification, the additional requirements are not onerous.

Implementing ISO 22301

The international standard for BCM, ISO 22301:2012 specifies requirements for setting up and managing an effective business continuity management system (BCMS). It is for use by internal and external parties, including certification bodies, to assess the organization's ability to meet regulatory and customer requirements as well as the organization's own requirements. ISO 22301 contains only those requirements that can be objectively audited and a demonstration of successful implementation can therefore be used by an organization to assure interested parties that an appropriate BCMS is in place.

During the latter part of 2012 or early in 2013, ISO will issue a guidance document: ISO 22313. This document will take the form of good practice guidance and recommendations, indicating what practices an organization should, or may, undertake to implement effective BCM. Organizations may choose to follow all or part of the guidance, which may be used for self-assessment or between organizations. The guidance is not a specification for BCM.

In common with modern management system standards, ISO 22301:2012 utilizes the PDCA (Plan-Do-Check-Act) cycle for developing, implementing and improving the effectiveness of an organization's BCMS.

Management systems approach – PDCA

The Plan-Do-Check-Act methodology is based upon the work of Walter Shewhart who developed statistical process control in the USA during the 1930s. It was taken up and promoted very effectively from the 1950s onwards by the famous quality management authority, W. Edwards Deming, and is used extensively to achieve continual improvement in management systems. Figure 2 shows the Shewhart or Deming cycle.

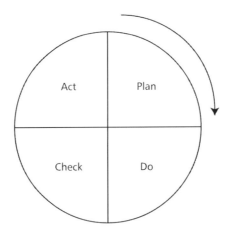

Figure 2 – The Shewhart or Deming cycle

Figure 3 shows how the PDCA cycle is applied to the BCMS as set out in ISO 22301. The PDCA model produces business continuity outcomes that meet the requirements and expectations of interested parties.

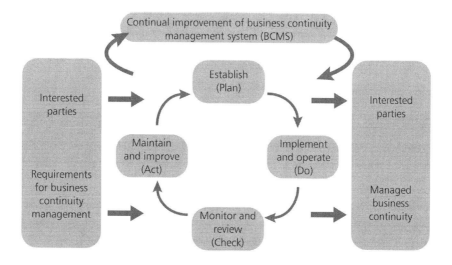

Figure 3 – Plan-Do-Check-Act cycle

Source: ISO 22301:2012

The elements of the PDCA cycle as it relates to BCM are as follows.

Plan (Establish)	Establish business continuity policy, objectives, targets, controls, processes and procedures relevant to improving business continuity in order to deliver results that align with the organization's overall policies and objectives.
Do (Implement and operate)	Implement and operate the business continuity policy, controls, processes and procedures.
Check (Monitor and review)	Monitor and review performance against business continuity policy and objectives, report the results to management for review, and determine and authorize actions for remediation and improvement.
Act (Maintain and improve)	Maintain and improve the BCMS by taking corrective action, based on the results of management review and reappraising the scope of the BCMS and business continuity policy and objectives.

Source: ISO 22301:2012

BCM, being a relatively new concept, will normally be introduced into a mature organization. The PDCA approach as used in ISO 22301 ensures there is a degree of consistency with other management system standards, such as BS EN ISO 9001:2008 (quality management systems) and BS EN ISO 14001:2004 (environmental management systems). If an organization already has an established management system to support these standards it may be sensible to base the BCMS on the same structures, in some cases providing an integrated management system.

Initial work by practitioners in 1999 resulted in a widely accepted representation of the BCM life cycle. With the publication of BS 25999-1 in 2006, a new illustration of the BCM life cycle was introduced. To align more closely, the diagram needs to be modified slightly as the maintaining and reviewing elements now relate closely to the BCMS (see Figure 4).

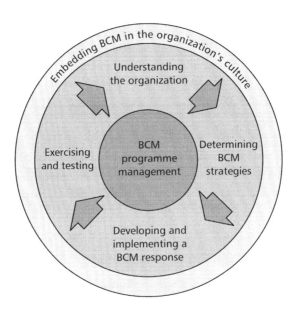

Figure 4 – The BCM life cycle

It is accepted that the PDCA approach can be applied to every element of the BCM life cycle but, for the purposes of this publication, the following approach has been taken.

Figure 4 could be described as the BCM wheel. The hub (BCM programme management) and the tyre (Embedding BCM in the organization's culture) are the elements that relate to Plan, Check and Act in the PDCA cycle. The spokes (Understanding the organization, Determining BCM strategies, Developing and implementing a BCM response and Exercising and testing) represent the Do element of the PDCA cycle.

At the heart of the BCM life cycle is programme management. It was given this title rather than project management because a project has a beginning and an end but BCM has to be seen as a continuous process. It should be considered as a programme of projects designed to ensure a current, relevant and assured BCMS exists within an organization. ISO 22301 defines a business continuity programme as being the 'ongoing management and governance process supported by top management and appropriately resourced to implement and maintain business continuity management'.

The elements of the BCM life cycle as they relate to ISO 22301 are as follows.

BCM programme management covers the following clauses of ISO 22301:

- 4 Context of the organization;
- 5 Leadership;
- 6 Planning;
- 7 Support;
- 8.1 Operational planning and control;
- 9 Performance evaluation; and
- 10 Improvement.

Understanding the organization relates to Clause 8.2 Business impact analysis and risk assessment.

Determining BCM strategies covers Clause 8.3 Business continuity strategy. The strategies chosen take into account existing business continuity and risk mitigation measures (Clause 8.3.3 Protection and mitigation).

Developing and implementing a BCM response covers Clause 8.4 Establish and implement business continuity procedures. This includes the establishment of an incident response structure and the creation of business continuity plans. A specific clause has been added to ISO 22301:2012 – 8.4.3 Warning and communication – that relates to the means for detecting and responding to an incident.

Exercising and testing covers Clause 8.5 Exercising and testing. The BCM life cycle in BS 25999-2 included maintaining and reviewing in this element of the cycle. These have now been incorporated into BCM programme management (see above).

Embedding BCM in the organization's culture relates to Clause 7.2 Competence and Clause 7.3 Awareness.

Comparing ISO 22301:2012 with BS 25999-2:2007

When news of an ISO standard for BCM emerged, business continuity managers expressed concern that they might have to radically rework their BCM procedures and processes once ISO 22301 was introduced. BS 25999-2 had been, and continues to be, used by many organizations across the world as the basis of their BCM procedures and processes. The good news is that BS 25999-2 has provided the main foundation of the new ISO standard. There are some important additions and a few elements that have been omitted. The additions have added greater depth and clarity while the omissions do not detract from the overall good BCM practices and principles.

The new standard is entitled *Societal security – Business continuity management systems – Requirements*. This is one of a suite of standards being developed by ISO/TC 223 designed to achieve greater societal security. Societal security can be defined as providing protection of society from, and the ability to respond to, incidents, emergencies and disasters caused by intentional and unintentional human acts, natural hazards, and technical failures.

The way in which ISO 22301 can be used is detailed in Clause 1 Scope. It states that the standard 'is applicable to all types and sizes of organizations that wish to

a)   establish, implement, maintain and improve a BCMS,
b)   ensure conformity with stated business continuity policy,
c)   demonstrate conformity to others,
d)   seek certification/registration of its BCMS by an accredited third party certification body, or
e)   make a self-determination and self-declaration of conformity with this International Standard [ISO 22301:2012].'

The standard can also be used by an organization to assess its suppliers' ability to meet continuity needs and obligations.

New concepts and activities have been introduced as follows.

Context of the organization	The environment in which the organization operates.
Interested parties	Replaces 'stakeholders'.
Leadership	Requirements specific to top management.

maximum acceptable outage (MAO)	'time it would take for adverse impacts, which might arise as a result of not providing a product/service or performing an activity, to become unacceptable'. This is the same as 'maximum tolerable period of disruption (MTPD)'.
minimum business continuity objective (MBCO)	'minimum level of services and/or products that is acceptable to the organization to achieve its business objectives during a disruption'.
Performance evaluation	Covers the measurement of BCMS and BCM effectiveness.
Prioritized timeframes	Order and timing of recovery for critical activities.
Warning and communication	Activities undertaken during an incident.

There have been many other additions and some slight alterations to the terms and definitions listed in the standard. The additions and changes reflect terms and definitions commonly used by BCM practitioners today.

The major additions to ISO 22301:2012 are as follows.

Clause 4 Context of the organization

This clause, covered in Chapter 3, introduces requirements necessary to establish the context of the BCMS as it applies to the organization, as well as needs, requirements and scope. ISO 22301 requires an organization to 'determine external and internal issues that are relevant to its purpose and that affect its ability to achieve the intended outcome(s) of its BCMS'. Understanding the organization and how it sits within its environment is an essential step to ensure any BCMS and BCM solutions developed are fit for purpose and relevant to the organization and interested parties.

This clause also requires the organization to determine its risk appetite and the legal and regulatory requirements that apply to the organization, and to clearly define the scope of the BCMS. Setting the initial scope of the BCMS is critical and must be done at an early stage. ISO 22301 requires the organization to determine what will be covered by business continuity and, just as importantly, what will be excluded. Scoping has presented challenges to many organizations seeking certification under BS 25999-2. Organizations are now required to clearly communicate the scope to relevant internal and external parties.

Clause 5 Leadership

Clause 5 summarizes the requirements specific to top management's role in the BCMS, and how they shall articulate their expectations to the organization via a policy statement.

New requirements are placed upon top management to demonstrate its commitment by

- 'ensuring that policies and objectives are established for the business continuity management system and are compatible with the strategic direction of the organization,
- ensuring the integration of the business continuity management system requirements into the organization's business processes,
- communicating the importance of effective business continuity management and conforming to the BCMS requirements'.

In addition it must ensure 'that the BCMS achieves its intended outcome(s)' and that it directs and supports continual improvement.

Policy creation and communication is an important element of Clause 5. It stresses the importance of ensuring the policy is appropriate to the organization, forms the basis for setting BCM objectives, and contains commitments to meeting legal and regulatory requirements and to continual improvement of the BCMS. It also states that the policy shall be available to appropriate interested parties.

Clause 5 requires top management to assign responsibility for the establishment, implementation and monitoring of the BCMS. What is missing is the requirement to appoint a specific sponsor from top management to 'champion' BCM in the organization. This is a regrettable omission as, to be successful, a BCMS must be introduced and supported by top management of the organization. Its involvement is required from the outset and its visible ongoing support is essential if BCM is to be taken seriously by the organization as a whole.

The requirements of Clause 5 are covered in Chapter 4.

Clause 6 Planning

This is a new section, covered in Chapter 5, and relates to establishing strategic objectives and guiding principles for the BCMS as a whole. The content of Clause 6 differs from establishing risk treatment opportunities stemming from risk assessment, as well as from the business impact analysis (BIA)-derived recovery objectives that are covered in Clause 8.

This section requires the organization to address the threats to the BCMS not being successfully established, implemented and maintained. It is about understanding the internal culture and the external environment in which the organization operates and the likely barriers that will prevent the BCMS being effective. It relates back to Clause 4.1 Understanding of the organization and its context and Clause 4.2 Understanding the needs and expectations of interested parties.

This clause requires the organization to clearly define the business continuity objectives and to have plans (projects) to achieve them. These objectives must tie back to the BCM policy and must be measurable. In setting the objectives account must be taken of the minimum level of products and services that will be acceptable to the organization in order to achieve its business objectives. Although it does not specify which products and services this applies to, it links back to the Scope (Clause 1) where the organization determined what would be covered by the BCMS. In BS 25999-2 these were referred to as the key products and services.

The organization must also determine who will be responsible for delivering the objectives, what will be done and in what timescale, what resources will be required and how results will be evaluated.

Clause 7 Support

Clause 7, covered in Chapter 6, details the support required to establish, implement and maintain an effective BCMS. This covers the resources required, the competence of those involved, awareness of, and communications with, interested parties, and requirements for document management.

BS 25999-2 requires a training needs analysis to be carried out to determine the gap between the competence required to fulfil appropriate BCM roles and the capabilities of those assigned to the roles. ISO 22301 does not specifically require such an analysis but does require an organization to ensure such persons are competent on the basis of education, training and experience.

The section covering awareness is more specific in that it requires all persons under the organization's control to be aware of the BCM policy, understand their contribution to the effectiveness of the BCMS and the implications of not conforming to its requirements. They must also understand their role at the time of disruption.

The major addition in Clause 7 covers communication, a vital part of managing any disruption and an area where many organizations fail. Clause 7.4 relates to internal and external communications and covers information about the BCMS and the organization's BCM capabilities, pre- and during disruption. It also sets out requirements for receiving and responding to communications from interested parties, adapting and integrating warning and informing systems and facilitating structured communications with appropriate authorities. It requires communications systems to be tested. Further requirements are also specified in Clause 8.4.3.

The requirements for BCMS documentation are more specific in ISO 22301:2012. It is essential that the organization fully documents all elements of the BCMS and business continuity procedures and that these documents are maintained, controlled and stored appropriately. This is particularly important for any subsequent audits required for compliance assessment or certification against ISO 22301.

Clause 8 Operation

Clause 8.1 Operational planning and control is a new clause and relates back to Clause 6.1, which requires the organization to identify the risks to the BCMS not being established, implemented and maintained by the organization. Clause 8.1 requires the organization to ensure processes that have been developed to manage the risks to the BCMS are being correctly implemented. This includes any processes that have been contracted-out or outsourced.

Clause 8.2.2 Business impact analysis introduces a new term, 'prioritized timeframes'; however, this is not listed in Clause 3 Terms and definitions. 'Prioritized timeframes' relates to the more familiar term, 'recovery time objective (RTO)', and defines the order and timing of recovery for critical activities that support the key products and services.

Although the term 'maximum tolerable period of disruption (MTPD)' is defined in Clause 3 it is not used in the body of the standard. However, Clause 8.2.2 c) does state that the organization must set prioritized timeframes for resuming activities that support the provision of (key) products and services 'at a specified minimum acceptable level, taking into consideration the time within which the impacts of not resuming them would become unacceptable'.

Clause 8.2.3 Risk assessment draws attention to the fact that 'certain financial or governmental obligations require the communication', at varying levels of detail, of the risks that could disrupt the prioritized activities. 'In addition, certain societal needs can also warrant sharing of this information', as appropriate.

Clause 8.4 Establish and implement business continuity procedures brings together all procedures necessary to deliver effective BCM procedures. The procedures must establish internal and external communications protocols, set out the immediate steps to be taken at the time of disruption but also be flexible to respond to changing circumstances and unanticipated threats. The BCM procedures must focus on impacts that could disrupt key products and services and be effective in minimizing the consequences of the disruption. This clause introduces the need to take account of stated assumptions and the organization's interdependencies.

Clause 8.4.2 Incident response structure has expanded requirements, namely the need to 'identify impact thresholds that justify initiation of formal response' and the need, using life safety as the first priority, to implement external warnings and communications as appropriate. This is covered in Clause 8.4.3 Warning and communication, which is an entirely new requirement.

Clause 8.4.4 Business continuity plans has fewer requirements than BS 25999-2. It does not require a named person to be designated as owner of the plan and be responsible for its review, update and approval. It does not require meeting locations and contact details to be included. It makes no specific reference to the need to include incident logs for recording decisions made and actions taken.

Clause 8.4.5 Recovery is an entirely new requirement. The standard simply states that 'The organization shall have documented procedures to restore and return business activities from the temporary measures adopted to support normal business requirements after an incident.' The looseness of this clause may lead to different interpretations across certification bodies.

Clause 8.5 Exercising and testing. ISO 22301 does not require an approved exercise programme to be in place. It does require the exercises to be based on an appropriate range of scenarios. It also links the review of the exercise back to the requirement to promote continuing improvement of the BCMS.

The requirements of Clause 8 are covered in Chapter 7.

Clause 9 Performance evaluation

This clause brings together the maintaining and reviewing of the BCMS. Chapter 12 covers this clause.

Clause 9.1 Monitoring, measurement, analysis and evaluation is a new set of requirements and is designed to ensure that appropriate metrics are in place to effectively manage the BCMS and provides the input to management reviews.

Clause 9.2 Internal audit now includes a requirement that the management responsible for the area being audited must 'ensure that any necessary corrections and corrective actions are taken without undue delay to eliminate detected nonconformities and their causes. Follow-up activities shall include the verification of the actions taken and the reporting of verification results.' Clause 9.2 drops the reference to taking into account the output of the BIA when developing an audit programme.

Clause 9.3 Management review is a very comprehensive clause. There is a new requirement to provide information for the review on the 'trends in

1.   nonconformities and corrective actions,
2.   monitoring and measurement evaluation results, and
3.   audit results'.

Additionally, when considering the output from the management review changes may be required to risk reduction and security arrangements and operational conditions and processes, if appropriate. It may also be appropriate to change the measures for 'how the effectiveness of controls are measured'.

This clause concludes with a requirement for the organization to

- 'communicate the results of [the] management review to relevant interested parties, and
- take appropriate action relating to those results'.

The management review no longer has to take input from interested parties or consider the results of training and awareness programmes.

Clause 10 Improvement

This clause combines the previous corrective and preventative actions under one heading: Nonconformity and corrective action.

A full cross-reference between BS 25999-2:2007 and ISO 22301:2012 is contained in Appendix B.

The rest of this book describes approaches that will enable those responsible for business continuity in an organization, regardless of size or sector, to meet the requirements of ISO 22301:2012.

Chapter 3   Context of the organization

No organization operates in a vacuum. There are many internal and external circumstances or factors that surround the organization that it must take into consideration when planning its approach to BCM and the development, implementation and maintenance of the BCMS.

Understanding the organization and its context

ISO 22301 requires an organization to determine the internal and external issues that are relevant to its purpose and affect its ability to achieve the expected outcomes of its BCMS. Understanding the organization and how it sits within its environment is an essential step to ensure any BCMS and BCM solutions developed are fit for purpose and relevant to the organization and interested parties.

Some of the analysis may already have been undertaken within the organization by risk or marketing managers. Those appointed to develop the BCMS for the organization can call upon the previous analysis to support this important stage. Alternatively they will need to work with appropriate top management and specialists to develop their own understanding.

The environment that surrounds and impacts upon an organization can be broken down into three areas, namely the 'internal environment', the 'micro environment' and the 'macro environment', as shown in Figure 5.

The internal environment

The first action is to identify the products or services that, if disrupted for any reason, would have the greatest impact upon the organization and its stakeholders and the achievement of the organization's goals and objectives. It is these products or services, often referred to as 'key', that initially will fall within the scope of the BCMS. Once BCM has been successfully established to deal with these key products or services there will be the opportunity to extend the scope to other areas of the organization. Initial discussion with top management will give an indication of which products and services are key for the organization.

In analysing the way key products or services are delivered an approach must be taken that breaks with the traditional functional view of the organization. A large multinational IT services company uses a methodology that considers what activities and functions are involved to get from 'quote to cash'. That is to say, what is needed to get into a position to quote against a tender, win the business, deliver to the customer's satisfaction, invoice for the goods and services delivered and subsequently receive payment. It requires an 'end-to-end' view of the organization and its activities, resources used and the role contributed by internal functions.

It is important to understand how decisions are made within the organization. What is its strategic direction and what are the policies and objectives that are in place to support the strategy? It is essential that any policy relating to BCM is linked to the organization's objectives and existing policies and procedures as appropriate. How is the organization structured and what governance arrangements exist? What is the approach to risk and what high-level risks face the organization?

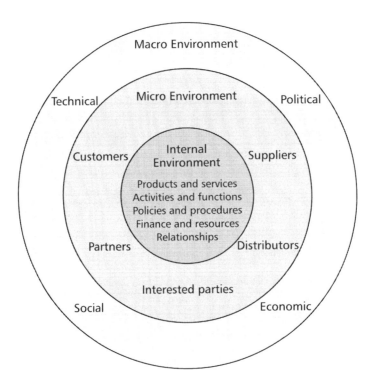

Figure 5 – The environment that surrounds and impacts upon an organization

All organizations have unique cultures, built up over time that influence the behaviours and actions of those involved. At the outset it is important to understand the culture and relationships that exist. Does a 'silo' mentality exist, is there a culture based on blame or is the organization open to new ideas and ways of working? Is the organization 'unionized'? Is it driven by dictate or consensus? If BCM is to be introduced successfully it must work with the culture.

The micro environment

The next step to consider is the micro environment surrounding the organization. The influencers here are customers, suppliers, partners, contractors, distributors and intermediaries. Does the organization have a few or many customers/clients? Does the organization deal direct with its customers/clients or does it operate through distributors and intermediaries, e.g. insurance brokers? Does it rely on a small number of suppliers? What contract arrangements and service-level agreements are in place with partners and outsourcing companies? Are there mutual aid arrangements in place? Who are the competitors and how do they operate in the marketplace?

The macro environment

It is important to understand how the pressures from the external environment can impact on an organization. Various analytical tools are available to assist in this, one of which is STEEPLE (see Figure 6).

Some of the questions that have to be answered for each element of the analysis are:

- What are the social responsibilities the organization has to the community, e.g. employment and/or safety? How does society view the activities of the organization, e.g. as a threat and/or with suspicion?
- How dependent is the organization upon external technologies, e.g. communications? How does the rapid advance in technology impact the organization, e.g. e-readers on book publishers?
- What is the economic climate in which the organization operates? What is the attitude towards debt by the financial institutions the organization is involved with? How strong are the economies of the countries in which and with whom the organization trades?
- What are the ethics of trade? What is the perception of the public and the media towards the organization and its activities, e.g. the use of child labour in the production process?
- What is the political climate in which the organization operates? Would a change of government affect attitudes towards the

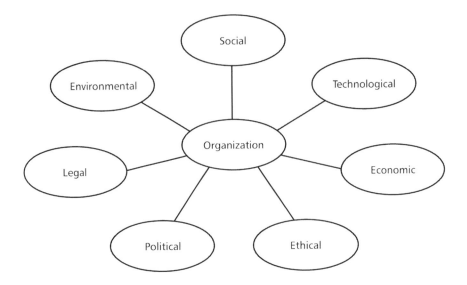

Figure 6 – STEEPLE

organization and its sector? What are the chances of terrorism and civil unrest affecting the organization?
- Which laws and regulations apply? Are they regional, national or international? ISO 22301 requires an organization to identify those laws and regulations that relate to the continuity of 'operations, products and services, as well as the interests of relevant interested parties'. The BCMS should be established, implemented and maintained taking into account the requirements of the applicable laws and regulations.
- And finally, what environmental considerations does the organization have to take account of? What is the organization's own impact on the environment, e.g. pollution? What are the external events that could impact the organization, e.g. from nature or from neighbours?

Having developed an understanding of the organization and the context in which it operates, the organization can develop specific BCM objectives. The high-level risks that the organization faces and the drivers that influence the decision to introduce business continuity arrangements will influence these objectives.

Understanding the needs and expectations of interested parties

When establishing the BCMS the organization must determine its relevant interested parties and understand their requirements, whether stated, implied or obligatory.

Interested parties are frequently referred to as stakeholders. These are individuals, groups of people or other organizations that can affect, be affected by, or perceive themselves to be affected by the decisions or activities of the organization, whether under normal operations or during a disruptive event, and can influence it but who may or may not be directly involved in undertaking the organization's activities.

Stakeholders can be classified into two groups:

1. primary stakeholders – these are usually internal stakeholders engaged in economic transactions with the organization. These include investors, customers, patients, contractors, suppliers, creditors and employees. Additional stakeholders include regulators, financial investors, banks, insurance companies and auditors.
2. secondary stakeholders – these are usually external stakeholders, who, although they do not engage directly with the organization, are affected by or can affect its actions. These include the general public, communities (both permanent and transitory), professional bodies, trade associations, government departments, activist groups and the media. The latter two can have considerable influence on the public's perception of the organization.

By understanding the stakeholders' interests in, and perceptions of, the organization under both normal and disruptive situations it is possible to develop appropriate continuity solutions that meet their needs and expectations. It is particularly important to develop appropriate strategies and plans to facilitate communications with interested parties at the time of disruption.

A simple technique that can be used to identify stakeholders and their expectations is to assemble a group of managers and get them to list the stakeholders and their expectations and then to rank the stakeholders in order of importance for the organization. The exercise has the additional benefit of helping the management team to look at the organization from the stakeholders' point of view rather than from within. Particular emphasis should be placed on the expectations of the customers and clients of the organization at the time of disruption.

A template for recording the results of the analysis of the interested parties' needs and expectations is included in Appendix C.

Determining the scope of the management system

The BCMS is the overarching management system that ensures BCM is correctly developed, implemented and maintained within an organization.

In designing the BCMS it is important to determine what will be included in the scope of the system as both internal and external parties need to understand what products, services and activities will be covered if the organization should suffer a disruptive event.

The needs and expectations of interested parties and the legal and regulatory requirements that apply to the organization will have a major influence upon the scope of the BCMS.

ISO 22301 states that 'the organization shall

a) establish the parts of the organization to be included in the BCMS,
b) establish BCMS requirements, considering the organization's mission, goals, internal and external obligations (including those related to interested parties), and legal and regulatory responsibilities,
c) identify products and services and all related activities within the scope of the BCMS,
d) take into account interested parties' needs and interests, such as customers, investors, shareholders, the supply chain, public and/or community input and needs, expectations and interests (as appropriate), and
e) define the scope of the BCMS in terms of and appropriate to the size, nature and complexity of the organization.'

A large and complex body is unlikely to introduce a BCMS for the entire organization at the initial pass but rather commence with the products and services that are key to meeting the objectives of the organization and the requirements of the external stakeholders. It may choose to introduce BCM to a specific location or function such as information and communications technology (ICT). A small organization is better able to encompass all of its activities first time round.

The organization must also identify and document those areas, products, services and activities that will not be covered by the BCMS scope. In doing so it is important to ensure that those activities excluded do not affect the organization's ability to deliver its key products and services.

Whatever the decision, it is vital that the scope of the BCMS is defined and documented at the outset of the programme. An example of a scoping document can be found in Appendix D. It is possible to include the scope within the policy document.

Chapter 4   Leadership

To be successful BCM must be introduced and supported by the organization's top management. Its involvement is required from the outset and its ongoing leadership and support is essential if BCM is to be taken seriously by the organization as a whole.

Top management must ensure that a BCMS is established that aligns with the strategic direction of the organization. BCM is not a bolt-on activity; it has to be integrated into business processes and must have the support of the staff across the organization. Top management needs to communicate why BCM is important, how it will be delivered and who will be responsible for the development, implementation and maintenance of the BCMS in the organization. This can be achieved by the publication of a BCM policy endorsed by top management.

Top management must recognize that effective BCM is not established overnight and that it is an ongoing activity. It must ensure that adequate resources are provided to enable the development of the BCMS and that staff appointed are competent and capable of delivering the required outcomes. In a large organization a dedicated BCM team may be appointed; in small- and medium-sized organizations BCM may be part of a single person's responsibilities.

Top management must agree what is to be covered by the BCMS with those appointed to run the system. It must also set out the organization's criteria for accepting risks and what levels of risk it is prepared to take. This should not just be its personal view but must also be influenced by the requirements and expectations of interested parties. Understanding of top management's approach to risk enables BCM staff to develop and implement BCM strategies that will be acceptable by top management. Without this criterion being set there is a danger that top management will reject proposed BCM strategies as being either overengineered or inadequate.

Top management's commitment does not end with the establishment of the BCMS. It must demonstrate its ongoing support by actively engaging in the exercising and rehearsing of business continuity plans, by ensuring that internal audits are conducted and by ensuring that the BCMS is subject to management reviews and continual improvement.

Setting the business continuity policy

The creation and publication of the organization's BCM policy document, signed by an executive director, is a key element of the BCMS and a clear demonstration of the organization's commitment.

The policy document should set out:

- the objectives for the establishment and maintenance of BCM within the organization;
- the scope of business continuity, including limitations and exclusions;
- an overview of the roles and responsibilities of those charged with delivering BCM;
- the resources allocated to BCM;
- the BCM principles, guidelines and standards that will apply;
- a reference to any legal or regulatory requirements; and
- the basis on which the BCMS will be measured, reviewed and continually improved.

The final point relates to how the organization assures itself that the BCMS is being correctly implemented and maintained within the organization. This is covered in Chapter 12.

The policy document should be brief and appropriate to the organization, taking into consideration the nature, scale, complexity, geography and criticality of its activities. It must also reflect the culture, dependencies and operating environment. If there is a standard format for policy documents in the organization then this should be followed.

The BCM policy document, once approved and signed off by top management, should be published within the organization and may be made available to appropriate interested parties. Key public sector bodies covered by the UK Civil Contingencies Act 2004 are required to make their BCM policy documents publicly available. These may be published on their websites or be available on request. There may be commercial advantage for private companies in similarly publishing their BCM policy documents. Listed companies could include reference to their policy in the annual report and accounts, providing assurance to investors and other interested parties that they take business continuity seriously.

The BCM policy, like all other policies within the organization, should be subject to regular review at an interval appropriate to the organization or when significant changes occur to the organization or the environment in which it operates. A sample policy document is included in Appendix E.

Roles, responsibilities and authorities

Executive management sits at the heart of effective BCM regardless of company size. All new management processes introduced to organizations require champions at a high level. This may be the managing director of a small company, a director of a major plc or an executive within a local authority who can take authority over, and accountability for, BCM and can demonstrate ongoing support for the initiative. A clear demonstration of this high-level commitment must be made across the organization at the very outset and must always be maintained.

An appropriate structure should be established that suits the organization.

A small organization may have a senior manager who has responsibility for the introduction and management of the BCMS. International businesses frequently have large teams that work throughout the world to establish and maintain BCM across the organization.

The level of BCM resources at the centre of the organization should be kept to the minimum and be appropriate to the size and geographical spread of the organization. BCM must be owned by the organization at the operational level. Creating a BCM department will enforce a 'silo' culture and undermine the inclusive principle that should be established through the belief that continuity is part of everyone's job. Figure 7 sets out a structure for a medium-sized organization. The BCM structures used within the organization must be clearly documented.

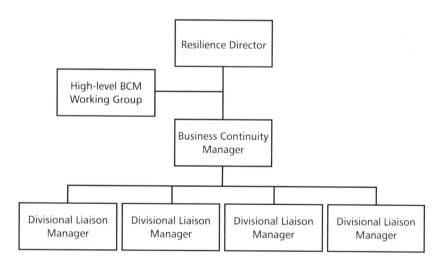

Figure 7 – Possible BCM structure

A high-level working group should be drawn from the senior management at division, product and/or service level. The role of the group is to:

- take overall control of resource allocation;
- set priorities for the organization;
- interpret the board's attitude towards risk;
- set continuity strategies in line with the organization's objectives and responsibilities;
- establish the measures that will be used to assure the BCMS remains current and relevant; and
- report to top management on the performance of the BCMS.

This group is also responsible for ensuring that the importance of BCM is communicated throughout the organization and that stakeholders are kept informed. The approach the high-level working group takes will have a strong influence on the culture within the organization. In a small organization this role may fall to the owner or managing director, who may be assisted by a senior employee. In a larger organization, divisional liaison managers are responsible for the introduction and maintenance of the BCM process within their area of operation. Very often these individuals have BCM added to their existing roles and responsibilities rather than being solely dedicated to the process.

Organizations that have successfully introduced BCM have used a 'matrix' management approach: a team of managers that understands the business and is able to appreciate how the organization operates, its activities and how it utilizes resources. Such teams may have representatives from the executive, operational management, legal, finance, technology (ICT), facilities, purchasing, security, human resources (HR), suppliers, etc. Their role is to advise the high-level working group throughout the BCM process.

Chapter 5   Planning

Actions to address risks and opportunities

There are many challenges facing organizations when introducing a new management system; BCMS is no different. It is important that those responsible for developing and introducing a BCMS should understand the challenges (risks) that will arise and develop plans and actions to counteract them.

It is vital to understand the organization's culture. It is important to gain an appreciation of the way the organization works, both formally and informally, and understand the experience gained from the introduction of other management systems or process changes that have already taken place. This provides an opportunity to build on what has been successful and develop appropriate plans and actions to overcome objections. BCM will have to be 'sold' to many people in the organization to gain their participation and support. Strong focus and leadership from the top is one of the prerequisites to ensuring BCM will be taken seriously.

It is important not to try to do too much at one time or to develop an overly complicated and comprehensive BCMS in the short term. Agree realistic expectations with top management, allowing sufficient time for the design phase of the BCMS. It is important to start small and limit the scope initially. If the introduction of the BCMS and BCM is to be sustainable, early efforts must be perceived as useful and as having organizational legitimacy. Therefore a gradual and systematic approach involving phased implementation is essential in most organizations.

Conflicting staff incentives can shift focus away from the BCMS, which can be seen as a nice-to-have process, towards the short-term objectives based on the must have, e.g. achievement of sales targets. Incorporating the implementation of the system into management objectives and ensuring these objectives are regularly reviewed will help focus management effort. Breaking down the implementation into realistic steps against which managers can be assessed will help.

It is important for top management to recognize the time and effort that will be required to develop and implement the BCMS. Agreeing realistic timescales and ensuring adequate resources are made available at the commencement of the project is important. It is vital to ensure those who are leading and involved in the process are adequately trained and competent.

Not all challenges will be internal. Changes in the laws and regulations that apply to the organization may force changes to the BCMS. The needs and expectations of those interested parties that are outside the organization may also influence the way that the BCMS is developed and implemented.

Organizations constantly change and organizational change affects every aspect of operations, including strategic planning, resource allocation and management, assessment and incentive systems, monitoring, and reporting. It is therefore vital to assess the BCMS against these changes to ensure it is still relevant and fit for purpose.

Business continuity objectives and plans to achieve them

Having identified the challenges and risks that surround the BCMS, top management must ensure that business continuity objectives are established, documented and communicated for relevant functions and levels throughout the organization.

The business continuity objectives must:

- be consistent with the business continuity policy;
- take account of the minimum level of products and services that is acceptable to the organization to achieve its objectives;
- be measurable;
- take into account applicable requirements of interested parties and laws and regulations;
- address the challenges and risks identified; and
- be monitored and updated as appropriate.

In setting the business continuity objectives, the organization must decide:

- who will be responsible for meeting each objective;
- what will be done;
- what resources will be required;
- the timescale in which the objective will be completed; and
- how the results will be evaluated.

As stated previously, consideration should be given to including BCM objectives in managers' personal objectives. Some organizations use an element of performance-related pay to ensure that BCM objectives have the right level of management focus.

One major UK telecommunications company has included an element of continuity in management objectives and has a comprehensive online training programme that all managers must undertake. A major London borough has gone one step further and linked BCM objectives to performance-related pay.

A forward-looking organization should include continuity in its mission/vision statement, e.g. 'to continue to be the most successful supplier of ....' If the management's key objectives are derived from the mission statement then they should also include continuity.

There should be clearly documented plans established to achieve BCM objectives. The use of project management tools and techniques is recommended with implementation plans set out as Program Evaluation and Review Technique (PERT) or Gantt charts. These can be subsequently submitted as evidence if the BCMS is subject to audit.

If the organization is dependent upon key suppliers, intermediaries or partners for the delivery of key products and services to its customers/clients then it is essential that any introduction of BCM acknowledges this, and the BCMS objectives and plans reflect the need to ensure the effectiveness of the key suppliers' or partners' BCM arrangements.

Chapter 6   Support

Resources

If the introduction and ongoing maintenance of BCM is to be successful then sufficient resources must be allocated to the programme. Top management frequently views BCM as a 'grudge purchase' and it requires a return on investment (ROI) to be demonstrated. This can be difficult as BCM is designed to maintain continuity in the unlikely event of a disruptive incident occurring.

The arguments for BCM are based more on economics than accountancy. It is the opportunity cost of failure that has to be weighed against the investments required. Examples of opportunity costs are the:

- cost to the organization, in lost sales, if production is disrupted for more than 'X' hours;
- financial penalties that will be incurred if the service/product cannot be delivered;
- value placed on lost customers if disruptions last more than 'X' days (taking into account that to win new customers is very expensive);
- value of lost contracts, or the inability to win new ones, as a result of being excluded for not having a BCMS in place; or
- fines or penalties that may be imposed for failing to meet applicable laws and regulations.

The level of resource required to implement and maintain a BCMS is appropriate to the size and nature of the organization and the environment in which it operates. For smaller organizations BCM does not have to be complex and appropriate BCM can be established at minimal cost. What is important is that sufficient time is allocated to those who are tasked with implementing the BCM programme. Once established, BCM should become part of normal business practice.

Training and competency

In Chapter 4 the importance of assigning roles and responsibilities was stressed; however, that is not enough. The organization must ensure that all personnel who are assigned business continuity roles and responsibilities are competent to perform the required tasks.

The tasks may be in BCMS development and planning or in an actual invocation following a major disruption. Under these circumstances people need to know what is expected of them and they must have the capabilities to perform the required tasks, often under stress. This is an area that can get overlooked. One major government department found that there were people named in its business continuity plans who did not know they were included and so had received no exposure to the roles and responsibilities and how to perform at the time of disruption.

BCM competence is a key element of ISO 22301 and BCM training is a statutory requirement placed on local government, emergency services and the NHS under the UK Civil Contingencies Act 2004. Financial resources must be set aside for this activity.

There are some key steps to be taken to ensure appropriate levels of BCM training and competencies exist within the organization. These are:

- determining the necessary competencies for those who will be tasked to work on BCMS (Appendix F contains a sample list of competencies);
- conducting training needs analysis on staff being assigned BCM roles and responsibilities in the development of the BCMS and those who will be involved when a plan is invoked;
- providing the training;
- evaluating the effectiveness of the training provided; and
- maintaining records of education, training skills, experience and qualifications.

Appendix G sets out a process for establishing a training programme.

If the organization does not have the staff resources or competent staff internally then it may hire or contract appropriate people. It is essential that the organization ensures that any such person has the necessary competence and experience to deliver the BCM programme.

Awareness

The outer part of the BCM life cycle (see Figure 4) relates to an organization's culture. To be successful, business continuity has to become part of the way that an organization is managed, regardless of size or sector. At each stage of the BCM process opportunities exist to introduce and enhance an organization's BCM culture.

ISO 22301 requires people doing work under the organization's control to be aware of:

- the business continuity policy;

- how they contribute to the effectiveness of the BCMS and achievement of the organization's business continuity objectives;
- 'the benefits of improved business continuity management performance';
- 'the implications of not conforming with the BCMS requirements';
- 'their own role during disruptive incidents'.

In order to achieve this awareness, the organization needs to raise, enhance and maintain awareness of the importance of BCM to the organization. This can be achieved by establishing an ongoing BCM education and information programme for all staff. It is important to introduce a process for evaluating the effectiveness of BCM awareness delivery.

Building, promoting and embedding a BCM culture within an organization ensures that it becomes part of the organization's core values and effective management.

An organization with a positive BCM culture will benefit, as it will:

- develop the BCM programme and the BCMS more efficiently;
- instil confidence in interested parties, especially staff and customers, in its ability to handle business disruptions;
- increase its resilience over time by ensuring BCM implications are considered in decisions made relating to existing products and services as well as to new ones; and
- minimize the likelihood and impact of disruptions.

Creating and embedding a BCM culture within an organization can be a lengthy and difficult process that might encounter a level of resistance that was not anticipated. An understanding of the existing culture within the organization will assist in the development of an appropriate BCM awareness programme.

To be effective, BCM must not be seen as a 'bolt-on' or as a 'passing initiative' from top management. Before the process can start, the board or executive team has to accept the importance and value of the BCMS process. It needs to encourage a management approach that contemplates the 'what ifs' or considers what might prevent delivery of the organization's products and/or services.

To be successful, BCM must be 'owned' by everyone within an organization. Many disruptions are caused by internal failures. Many organizations have a blame culture that prevents people from flagging up problems. If the culture is about only wanting to hear the 'good news' then there will be a reluctance to draw attention to failings, which may subsequently lead to disruptions and eventual crises for the organization.

All staff, including middle management, must be convinced that BCM is a serious issue for the organization and that they have an important role to play in maintaining the delivery of products and services to their clients and customers. It is essential that awareness programmes be established as part of the overall introduction of BCM.

Raising awareness is done in two stages. The first is to ensure that all those in the organization are aware BCM is being introduced and why. They will need to be convinced that this is a lasting initiative that has the support of the executive.

> Novartis, an international pharmaceutical company, issues every member of staff with a Code of Conduct. In a section headed 'Business Continuity', it states:
>
> > We believe that business continuity management is critical for our patients, customers, associates and other stakeholders, and is part of responsible management practice. In the event of an emergency or significant business disruption, we are committed to doing our utmost to ensure uninterrupted supply of key products and services.
> >
> > Source: Novartis Employee Code of Conduct, 2011
>
> The code, which is signed by the Chairman and CEO, sets out what is expected of the individual employee, stating:
>
> > Our Code of Conduct reflects our commitments to meet the expectations of our stakeholders as a responsible corporate citizen and contains the fundamental principles and rules concerning ethical business conduct.
>
> The code provides a link to other materials on the company's intranet site.

A technique that was used very successfully in the introduction of total quality management in the 1980s was to hold team meetings at each level of the organization to introduce the concept and to ask the team to consider how it could improve the quality of its output.

The same principle can be applied to BCM, with the teams being asked to identify aspects that prevent or impede the continuity of their areas of operation. The key questions to ask are the 'what ifs' since this style of question gets the group thinking about its contribution to continuity. Experience has shown that, even at the lowest level, employees are able to relate to the BCM concept and not only identify areas of potential disconnect but also possible solutions that can maintain continuity.

Each organization will have a level of management that is particularly sceptical about the introduction of new initiatives; this is very often middle management. Particular emphasis must be given to gaining its support if BCM is to become part of the organization's culture. This management level will also have a large part to play in the initial charting of critical processes and activities, so gaining its support at an early stage is vital.

The second stage of raising awareness occurs once the business continuity plans have been produced. It is important that appropriate interested parties are made aware that the organization has such plans in place. This will help to raise their level of confidence in the organization's ability to deal with disruptions.

Employees need to have confidence that their jobs will be protected while the disruption is being contained. It is also critical that individuals know what actions they are required to take when the plan is invoked.

> A major UK retailer has a communications policy that is designed to ensure its employees know what to do if an incident occurs. They are given a number to call if they become aware of an incident at work or they see a news report, etc. concerning a disruption at their work location. When one of its London stores caught fire the employees knew what to do the next day. Some went to previously designated alternative locations; others remained at home and called the staff helpline for recorded advice.
>
> Lesson: ensure employees are kept informed about what is needed from them at the time of disruption.

Employees new to an organization must be made aware of the BCM policy and their part in the business continuity process. This can be accomplished by incorporating BCM material into the staff induction programme. Awareness of the BCMS can be maintained by using internal newspapers, emails, the organization's intranet, team meetings and broadcasts from senior management. These may highlight examples where the organization successfully managed an incident, praising those involved. It may also draw upon lessons learned from the failures of other organizations.

A good awareness programme will have the effect of making all staff understand the significance of 'thinking continuity' in their everyday activities. For example the purchasing department in the organization has an important role to play in ensuring that key suppliers are made aware of the importance of BCM to the organization and the processes they should adopt to ensure continuity of supply. This applies to existing and new supply contracts.

Those responsible for new product development should be encouraged to build continuity solutions into the design of the product and its supporting processes. It is easier and more cost-effective to design in continuity at the concept stage than to add it as a bolt-on after a problem has arisen. One Australian bank will not allow a product to be launched onto the market unless an appropriate continuity solution has been incorporated.

All staff must understand that BCM is a serious issue for the organization and that they have an important role to play in maintaining the delivery of products and services to its clients and customers.

Communication

One of the biggest challenges to any organization suffering a disruptive incident is the need to maintain communications with interested parties.

There are many cases of companies that have believed they managed a disruptive incident well and minimized the impacts on the organization. What then disappoints them is the reaction of the external community following restoration of service and supply. What they failed to do was to recognize the importance of communicating with all the interested parties, both internally and externally.

When a company that manufactured PCs to order had problems loading the operating system software onto its product, it correctly stopped the production line in order to prevent faulty machines being delivered to its customers. The company chose not to inform customers of the problem unless they contacted it directly. Disgruntled customers contacted the main IT newspaper, which picked up the story and ran it the following week, damaging the company's reputation in the process.

Lesson: if you intend to do nothing then make certain you have informed those who are expecting service or product delivery.

Particular emphasis should be placed on communication with staff, as they will be concerned about their welfare and employment. At the time of disruption clear communication is required to advise staff of what actions to take. This can be done through hard copy, email, the organization's intranet, local media or recorded messages on a freephone number.

It should be recognized that communications will be a two-way process and arrangements must be made for staff to be able to flag up incidents or leave messages about their own situation, e.g. checking in if there are major transport disruptions due to bad weather.

Arrangements must be made to keep senior management informed about the progress towards resumption. It is essential to identify who within the organization will be responsible for planning and delivering communication.

One key element of a communication strategy is how the organization will manage the media at the time of a major disruption. Regardless of the size of the organization, if the event is significant enough to raise the media's interest a competent person must be appointed to act as the organization's spokesperson. Preparing material that can be quickly adapted when needed will save time. This should include draft response statements and general information about the organization. How this is managed must be developed as part of the communication strategy.

It is important that those responsible for handling media communications monitor what is actually reported in the press and on radio and TV. If the reports are positive then subsequent messages released should build on this; if the reports are negative the organization has to consider how, and if, the negatives are counteracted.

The emergence of social media, e.g. blogs, Facebook and Twitter, offers new opportunities to provide fast communications to staff, the public and other key parties, e.g. suppliers. If it is intended to use these channels then their limitations and accessibility to the wider community must be recognized. It is important to monitor social media to see what the public, and interested parties, is saying about the organization's disruption and how it is being handled. Messages posted by individuals on Twitter can spread very quickly. The death of an international singer in 2012 reached 2.5 million people across the world in two hours. In 2012 it has been estimated that 750 million people use social media daily and/or weekly.

It is not just about having the processes and procedures in place when things go wrong. It is also about raising the awareness of interested parties of what the organization has in place to manage disruptions.

Customers will need to know how their supply of goods and services will be affected and when they can expect a return to normal working practices. Suppliers will need to know the alternative locations they will be required to deliver supplies to and also will need to be confident that they will be paid. The banks and investors will need to have confidence in the management being able to handle the disruption effectively and will need to know their investments are safe.

Regulators, legislators and others with statutory responsibilities will need to understand the alternative arrangements that will be in place to meet the organization's statutory and regulatory requirements. The wider community may need to be informed of actions that will be taken if the disruption could have a serious impact on their welfare, e.g. warning the public in the event of a chemical plant fire.

ISO 22301 places great importance on the role of communications in business continuity. It requires organizations setting up their BCMS to determine the need for both internal and external communications. This must cover what and when to communicate and to whom it will communicate.

ISO 22301 states that 'the organization shall establish, implement, and maintain procedure(s) for

- internal communication amongst interested parties and employees within the organization,
- external communication with customers, partner entities, local community, and other interested parties, including the media,
- receiving, documenting, and responding to communication from interested parties,
- adapting and integrating a national or regional threat advisory system, or equivalent, into planning and operational use, if appropriate,
- ensuring availability of the means of communication during a disruptive incident,
- facilitating structured communication with appropriate authorities and ensuring the interoperability of multiple responding organizations and personnel, where appropriate, and
- operating and testing of communications capabilities intended for use during disruption of normal communications.'

When planning the communications element of the BCMS the organization should use the output of the stakeholder analysis that formed part of establishing the context of the organization.

Documented information

Proving that a BCMS is effective is one of the key challenges facing any organization. Documents should be kept relating to the management of the BCMS and of exercises, incidents, outcomes, lessons identified and actions taken. For those seeking certification to ISO 22301 there is a clear requirement to establish a documented management system and such documentation will provide significant evidence when an organization is audited for certification.

Evidence from such documents can be used to demonstrate to internal management that the policy is adhered to and objectives are being met. The outcomes and lessons learned from exercises and incidents will help to justify the investment made in BCM to the top management of the organization.

External stakeholders will also be interested in such documents. In the event of an inquiry or legal claim being mounted against an organization that has experienced a major incident and failed to maintain the supply of critical products and/or services, evidence will be required of how the BCMS operates in the organization and how the incident was managed. Being unable to produce such evidence may harm the organization.

A major element of any management system is the control and management of documentation. With BCM this is critical since, at the time of any disruption, it is essential that all players have access to, and work from, authorized and current incident or continuity plans and supporting documentation. Much of the information contained within the BCMS documentation will be of a sensitive nature and therefore must be subject to appropriate protection and confidentiality markings.

Creating and updating documentation

ISO 22301 requires the management of the organization to establish and maintain a process for creating and updating documented information that covers:

a) 'identification and description (e.g. a title, date, author or reference number),
b) format (e.g. language, software version, graphics) and media (e.g. paper, electronic), and review and approval for suitability and adequacy'.

The extent of the documented information required for a BCMS will be dependent upon the size and nature of the organization, the complexity of its business and the people involved.

Documentation required

The organization must have documentation covering the following aspects of the BCMS:

- the context of the organization;
- the needs and expectations of interested parties;
- the legal and regulatory requirements;
- the scope of the BCMS, including exclusions;
- evidence of top management commitment;
- BCM policy;
- BCM organization, roles and responsibilities;
- BCM objectives and plans to achieve them;
- the procedures in support of the BCMS;
- the monitoring and measurements to assess the BCMS and the subsequent results;
- BCM competence requirements, staff assessments and training records;
- internal and external BCMS communication plans and delivery records;
- BIA and risk assessment processes;
- the outputs from the business impact analyses and risk assessments;
- the BCM strategies;
- incident, business continuity and recovery management processes and plans;
- up-to-date contact and mobilization details for personnel and any relevant agencies, organizations and resources that might be required to support the response strategies;
- an exercise schedule, results and actions;
- post-incident reviews and actions;
- audit schedules, results and actions;
- BCMS management reviews and actions; and
- document management processes.

The extent of documented information can differ among organizations. It will depend upon the size of the organization, its operations and its interdependencies. Any organization that is subject to audit, either voluntarily or as a result of a mandatory requirement, will be required to provide documentary evidence relating to its BCMS. The above list provides a useful guide to appropriate documentation. Those wishing to be certified to ISO 22301 will have to adhere to this list as a minimum.

Control of documented information

Documented information required by the BCMS must be subject to controls that cover its:

- protection, distribution and access (includes levels of access rights);

- storage and preservation, including legibility;
- retrieval and use;
- version control and prevention of unintended use of obsolete information;
- preservation; and
- retention and disposal.

Not all documented information required for the planning and operation of the BCMS may be held within the organization. If this is the case it is necessary to identify the location and, as appropriate, for it to be controlled.

Any documentation required by the BCMS must be protected to ensure that no unauthorized modifications or deletions can be undertaken.

Chapters 3 to 6 covered the Plan element of the BCMS, incorporating the policy, structure, resources, training and assurance, as set out in the hub (programme management) and the tyre (culture) of the BCM life cycle, shown in Figure 4. Chapter 7 looks at the Do element of the PDCA cycle.

Chapter 7   Operation

This section covers the Do element of the PDCA cycle. Its purpose is to define business continuity requirements, determine how to address them and develop the procedures to manage a disruptive incident. In relation to the BCM life cycle (see Figure 4) this section includes:

- understanding how the organization delivers key products and services;
- determining business continuity strategies;
- developing and implementing a BCM response; and
- exercising.

Many organizations start by developing continuity plans against perceived risks such as loss of IT services or building facilities. This is the traditional disaster recovery approach, which delivers a degree of comfort to senior managers in that something has been done to protect the organization. However, it has an inherent problem in that it might overlook critical activities outside these services and facilities and not meet the actual needs of the business.

The direction that BCM has now taken is based on ensuring the continuity of critical processes and activities that deliver key products and services to clients and customers. This is more aligned with total quality management, which is based on supplier/customer relationships and the processes that serve them.

Every organization has inputs and outputs regardless of size, sector or type, whether it is a commercial business, public body, voluntary organization or charity. All have customers or clients to whom they deliver products or services. The drivers for the organization to deliver these products and services may be different, e.g. profit, community service, legislation or regulation. They will vary from sector to sector and are dependent on the size of the organization. In addition there are many stakeholders who have a keen interest in what the organization delivers and how the products and services are produced. The requirement to identify the interested parties and their needs and expectations was covered in Chapter 3 as part of the Plan element of the PDCA cycle.

Operation planning and control

The start of Chapter 5 covered the requirement for an organization to establish actions to address risks and opportunities to the BCMS and, where applicable, integrate and implement these actions into the BCMS processes. As the organization develops the BCM processes that will protect the continuity of key products and services, it must ensure that the appropriate controls are carried out as planned whether these are in-house, contracted out or outsourced.

BIA and risk assessment

These two activities are of the greatest importance, being the basis on which the business continuity procedures are to be built. The organization must ensure that sufficient time and resources are allocated to these tasks and that the staff who are to undertake them are competent and adequately trained. Some organizations choose to use external consultants to facilitate this work but it must be recognized that it is the individuals who deliver the key products and services who actually understand how the processes and activities work and what resources and dependencies support them.

ISO 22301 (Clause 8.2.1) requires an organization to 'establish, implement and maintain a formal and documented process for business impact analysis and risk assessment that

a)   establishes the context of the assessment, defines criteria and evaluates the potential impact of a disruptive incident,
b)   takes into account legal and other requirements to which the organization subscribes,
c)   includes systematic analysis, prioritization of risk treatments, and their related costs,
d)   defines the required output from the business impact analysis and risk assessment, and
e)   specifies the requirements for this information to be kept up-to-date and confidential.'

Impact versus risk

The standard does not specifically indicate in which order the BIA and risk assessment should be undertaken. The traditional risk management approach would be to consider the threats/risks that could disrupt the critical activities that support key products or services and what can be done to prevent them.

BCM on the other hand adopts an approach based on impact and time. It looks at the impact on the organization if critical activities are interrupted; it looks at effects rather than causes. While we can predict many threats, recent occurrences have shown that the unexpected can always happen, e.g. fuel shortages, the floods of 2007 and the loss of water supplies that resulted from them, the volcanic ash cloud that closed European air space and the Japanese earthquake, tsunami and nuclear accident.

As stated before, BCM requires the organization to consider what the impact would be on itself and its interested parties if the delivery of key products or services, the processes used and their supporting critical activities were disrupted for any reason.

Defining key products and services

There are two ways to identify the key products and services of an organization. The first involves seeking input from operational management on what it considers is important to the organization. The results are collated and an attempt is made to rank the activities in order of priority for resumption. The danger in taking this approach is that many operational managers naturally see their own areas of operation as critical and ranking will be difficult. It is also possible that when the analysis is presented to top management it may disagree on the findings.

The second, and preferred, approach is to use a senior management team – this may be a BCM high-level working group – to consider the organization as a whole and to provide a prioritization for key products or services. In doing so it must take into consideration the needs and expectations of the interested parties and the legal and other requirements that apply to the organization, which should already have been identified. This approach provides the quickest route to establishing the first element of BCM implementation.

A complex organization may have many products and services and, while all are important, some are more critical than others. For example, one UK county council delivers more than 200 services to the community. Following the high-level consultation it was established that 37 of these activities were key or vital for the community. With this knowledge the council concentrated its BCM activities on the most important areas for the authority and the community.

Once the key products and services have been identified the next task is to determine the point at which the MTPD occurs for each product and service. The MTPD is defined in ISO 22301 as the 'time it would take for adverse impacts, which might arise as a result of not providing a product/service or performing an activity, to become unacceptable'. An alternative definition given in BS 25999-2 is that it is the duration after which the organization's viability will be irrevocably threatened if the product or service cannot be resumed.

Measures of impact could be:

- financial loss;
- the impact on service delivery;
- embarrassment or loss of reputation;
- threat to personal safety;
- personal privacy infringement;
- failure to meet statutory or regulatory obligations; or
- effect on project objectives and schedules.

The measures chosen must be appropriate: those for a commercial organization may be different from those for a public body.

An example of a business impact assessment matrix is shown in Appendix H.

Some products or services and their supporting processes and activities are more critical at certain points in the calendar, e.g. key reporting dates, elections, payment dates (including payroll), school admissions, events associated with festivals and gritting of roads. In addition there may be key projects that have to be delivered on time and, if disrupted, will have serious consequences for the organization. As we cannot predict when any disruption will occur it is essential to chart these activities/events against a calendar (see Figure 8).

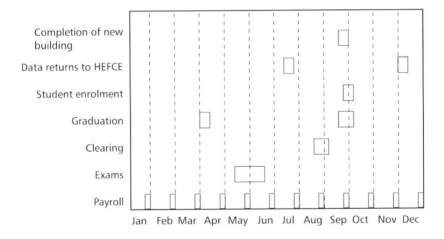

Figure 8 – Key annual events for an English university

It is important to prioritize timescales for resumption of a product or service within the MTPD. This is called the recovery time objective (RTO) and it specifies the point in time by when resumption must be achieved.

In some cases the organization may require a phased restoration, building towards full recovery. The organization must also determine the minimum acceptable levels at which key products or services must be resumed by the recovery deadlines. This is called the minimum business continuity objective (MBCO). Top management should agree the list of key products and services, their MTPDs, RTOs and MBCOs.

Appendix I provides a template for this stage of the BIA.

The output from these consultations is used to identify the critical processes and activities, together with their supporting resources and dependencies, that enable the organization to deliver its key products and services. Consideration must also be given to any third party's role in these processes and activities. Third parties include suppliers, outsourcers and intermediaries (see Figure 9).

As their contract is with the organization, customers or clients will expect the organization to deliver the product or service regardless of the ability of the other players to maintain their continuity of operations. They will hold the organization responsible for failure.

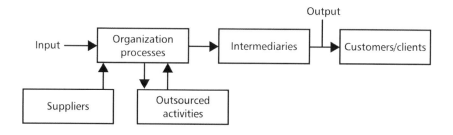

Figure 9 – The end-to-end view of delivery

As an example consider home care for the elderly. Local authorities are increasingly using third parties to deliver this service. However, if the service fails or is below standard it will not be the third-party intermediary that the client or their relatives will hold responsible but the local authority in whose name the service is being delivered. It is therefore essential that the local authority ensures the intermediary has effective BCM in place.

Michael Porter's value chain analysis (Porter, 1985) provides a useful methodology to assist in the understanding of how an organization works. The activities are broken down to ascertain where value is added. This provides a starting point in understanding how the organization works. Many senior managers make the assumption that they 'know how it works around here'. This is often not the case as the investigation into many disasters has clearly shown. If it is not understood how the organization works 'normally' then there is little chance of keeping it running at a time of a crisis.

Process mapping

Having gained the agreement of the high-level working group or top management as to which are the key products or services, the next stage is to identify the critical activities that support these products and services.

Activities, some formal, some informal, that have been established over time will support the critical processes. They all draw upon the resources of the organization and of third parties. The next stage is to identify these activities and the resources they use.

Process mapping should now be undertaken on the critical activities. The benefit of using this technique is that it will identify what actually happens in the organization in order to deliver the key products or services. The most dangerous step to take at this stage is for managers to assume they know how things are done in the organization. Managers that have risen through the organization usually lose touch with practices on the ground. It is vital that we understand what actually happens in order to replicate this at the time of any disruption in order to provide a seamless continuity of operations. If it is not understood how the organization works 'normally' then there is little chance of keeping it running at a time of crisis.

It is possible that this has already been carried out in the organization. If so, the outputs should be examined to see if they are still current and relevant to BCM.

As an example consider the fictitious Acme Organization Ltd that delivers a range of facility management services. It has four main customer-facing divisions: Home Service, Estate Management, Domestic Installations and Commercial Contracts. These are supported by internal departments, including purchasing, which also run the stores' facilities for spares and equipment (see Figure 10).

Top management considers emergency call-outs to be a key service for the home-based customer, as this is a contracted service to the local housing association. The critical processes and activities, and the supporting resources, now need to be identified together with any internal or external dependencies. This has to be done on an end-to-end basis for the whole service, from reception of call through to resolution; this is what the customer expects from the organization.

The mapping starts with the high-level processes, e.g. dealing with a domestic customer's faulty heating system (see Figure 11).

The next level down is then mapped (see Figure 12).

There may be further levels of activities below these that also need to be recorded. The system used to record the activities may be paper-based or an appropriate software package.

The individuals who operate the processes and activities should be involved in helping to map the way they work and the resources they use. Because people work in different ways and informal activities develop over time it is useful, where possible, to work with several people who are involved in operating the same activity.

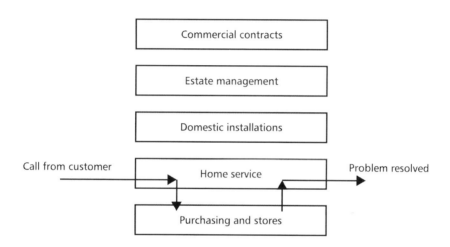

Figure 10 – Handling a home emergency call-out

Figure 11 – High-level process mapping example

The process mapping exercise opens up an opportunity for those delivering the service to raise areas where they experience difficulties: perhaps through the lack of resources, failure of supply, or breakdown in systems and security. They should also be asked about how they currently overcome disruptions to the activity. Input at this level can identify

Figure 12 – Detailed process mapping example

continuity solutions – workarounds that already exist but may not be documented and also areas where the organization can be made more resilient by reducing vulnerabilities.

A process mapping tool

One simple form of process mapping is based on the use of adhesive notes. The person who undertakes the activity is interviewed on what they do. The interviewer writes each stage of the activity on a separate adhesive note, which is then attached to a flip chart (see Figure 13). The use of adhesive notes allows missed steps to be added without having to redraw the flow diagram. Very often those being interviewed miss out steps as they assume the interviewer knows what happens next.

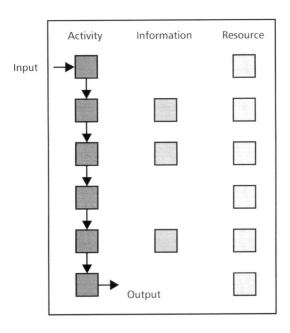

Figure 13 – Simple process mapping

The next stage is to use different-coloured adhesive notes to chart resources used against stages in the activity. The key resources used to support the activities may be people, information systems (ICT), facilities and suppliers. The number, location, skills, roles and responsibilities of the people required should be noted. The systems that support them must be logged, e.g. computer hardware, software applications, telecommunications and information (data). It should be noted what facilities in terms of premises, plant, machinery and materials are required. Very often third parties have a major role to play in critical activities as suppliers of goods and services, as outsourcers or as agents between the organization and its customers or clients. Their part must be recorded.

As information is so important to the operation of any activity it is recommended that a separate line and colour of adhesive note is used for information sources. When the mapping exercise is complete the output should be permanently recorded.

When the mapping has been completed for all the activities that support the critical processes for key products or services, it is possible to identify all the resources and functions that are used to support these activities (see Figure 14).

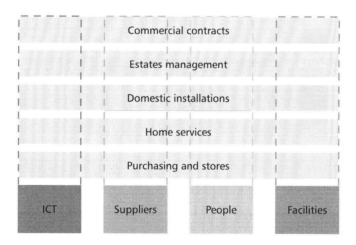

Figure 14 – Mapping resources to critical activities

The inputs and outputs are recorded together with the timescales and the resources used to complete the activity. The resources are recorded against the individual activity element. As previously stated, it is important to recognize that some activities are seasonal and that the use of resources may vary throughout the year, e.g. Christmas mail sorting and delivery requires temporary staff and additional facilities.

Appendix J provides a template for recording resources against activities.

Risk assessment

It is now possible to undertake risk assessments against the resources identified from the process mapping. If the organization has an established risk management process in place it is sensible to use this process for the BCM risk assessment. Single points of failure (SPoFs) exist in every organization, e.g. a key member of staff, building or supplier. Using the data from the process mapping exercise, it is easier to identify which processes and hence which activities will be affected by a single point of failure.

A manufacturer in the North East of England made a range of office furniture. One factory line produced a high-volume, low-profit margin, general office range while another made the executive range in low volumes but with high margins. It was the company's ability to supply both ranges that resulted in contracts with major organizations. When analysing the risks to the executive range it was realized that the production line had a single point of failure. It had only one, very elderly, employee who was capable of applying the wood veneers to this key range of furniture and without him the line would stop. Failure to deliver the executive furniture to the organizations could result in the loss of the general office furniture contract with those companies.

Lesson: identify SPoFs and ensure you have an appropriate risk treatment in place.

Internal and external threats, liabilities and exposures are identified, together with the likelihood of the threat occurring. The results must be recorded. A risk register may already exist as part of the organization's risk management system and consideration should be given to establishing one integrated risk register.

Consideration must also be given to disruptions and crises that occur outside the organization. In addition the failure of a competitor can rebound on other organizations in the same industry. The capsizing of the *Costa Concordia* off Tuscany in January 2012 not only impacted the ultimate owners, Carnival Corporation, but also potentially reduced overall demand across all cruise companies.

The 2005 product recall of more than 600 food lines from UK shops containing Worcester sauce contaminated with Sudan 1 (a carcinogenic food colouring) affected sales of Lea & Perrins® Worcestershire Sauce despite this product containing no artificial colouring. Name association by the media and the public resulted in depressed demand for the Lea & Perrins® product. Three thousand five hundred customers called the Lea & Perrins® helpline in the first four days of the product recall requiring it to draft in extra staff. The company had to launch an expensive advertising campaign to protect the brand and its 90 per cent market share.

Lesson: it might not be an incident that directly occurs within your control that threatens your organization. The perceptions of interested parties, in this case the wider public, must be taken into account when developing BCM procedures.

The results of the BIA and risk analysis are then used to create a risk matrix for the critical activities as shown in Figure 15.

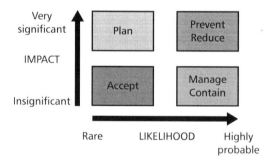

Figure 15 – Example of a risk matrix

The high-level working group or top management is again consulted to seek agreement on the assignment of the risks to the critical activities. Its decision must take account of the organization's risk appetite that was established when the BCMS project was commenced. This will determine the level of resilience required and the amount of delay that is acceptable before continuity of operations is achieved.

Risk treatments for protection and mitigation

From the risk assessment matrix in Figure 15 it can be seen that there are a number of options that can be applied to the critical activities: accept, manage or contain, reduce or prevent, and plan. An appropriate risk treatment may be to implement one or a combination of these.

Accept

Where the impact would be insignificant and the likelihood of failure is rare the high-level working group may decide to accept the risk and do nothing. This is a perfectly acceptable course of action and is driven by the risk appetite of the organization. The risk appetite will vary according to the size and style of the organization, the stakeholders and their interests, the sector in which it operates, the behaviour of competitors and the senior management's own approach to risk.

Mitigate

Where the risk level is high but the impact on the critical activity would be low the best option is to mitigate the risk, which is to say, manage or contain the risk. If the risk of power failure is high then the provision of a standby generator and uninterrupted power supply will minimize the impact on critical activities. If the use of a single supplier would stop the activity then a second supplier would provide appropriate resilience to minimize the risk.

Stop, cease or suspend

Where the likelihood of failure is very high and the impact would be considerable on the organization, urgent action will be needed. If it is not possible to reduce the risk then a decision may be taken to cease the activity. This may not be possible if it is a statutory requirement, e.g. to fight fires. Alternatives are to change or re-engineer the processes that support the activities or to transfer to an alternative location where the risk may be lower, e.g. move away from a flood plain.

Plan for continuity

Where the risk of failure is low but the impact would be high it is essential that consideration be given to continuity management plans that could deal with such a situation if it should arise. An example would be the case of a group of key staff winning The National Lottery and all deciding to leave their jobs immediately.

Appendix K provides a template for recording risks and mitigation strategies.

Insurance is often seen as a way of offsetting the consequences of some threats if they should occur. Although insurance can compensate for loss of facilities and earnings it will not protect brand and reputation. Customer loyalty cannot be taken for granted and therefore organizations will have to consider how they will retain clients and customers until full service is restored.

Business continuity planning is an element of the BCM process that is designed to ensure the organization can continue to deliver its key products and services to clients and customers. The depth of planning applied depends upon the level of risk and impact on the organization that it is prepared to accept as a result of a disruption, based on its risk appetite.

The outcome of the risk assessments should be a set of risk treatments that is designed to

a) 'reduce the likelihood of disruption,
b) shorten the period of disruption [if it should happen], and
c) limit the impact of disruption on the organization's key products and services'.

Both BIA and risk analysis must be reviewed at planned intervals and when significant changes occur to the organization or the environment in which it operates.

Chapter 8   Business continuity strategies

Having identified the critical activities and resources that support the key products or services of the organization, completed the impact and risk assessments and agreed the prioritized RTOs, together with the minimum level of operation required, it is time to consider how continuity will be achieved.

ISO 22301 states that the organization must determine and select appropriate strategies for:

a)   'protecting prioritized activities,
b)   stabilizing, continuing, resuming and recovering prioritized activities and their dependencies and supporting resources, and
c)   mitigating, responding to and managing impacts'.

Those responsible for BCM must determine how the organization will recover each critical activity within its RTO and what resources will be required; this will generate a continuity resource requirement statement. In addition they must determine how relationships with key stakeholders will be managed at the time of disruption. In choosing the appropriate options or strategies, consideration must be given to the MTPD for each activity, the costs of implementing the strategy and the consequences of inaction.

In setting the strategies, consideration must be given to how they will utilize key resources, e.g. people, premises, facilities, equipment and consumables, ICT, transportation, finance, supplies, and information and data. Information was considered separately from technology in undertaking the process mapping outlined in Chapter 7. If the ICT fails, being able to gain manual access to critical information might enable critical activities to continue.

> A company in the South East of the UK was an important supplier of an essential product to a large meat processor in East Anglia. Its factory was located in a small town and the power to the factory was from the only electricity substation in the area. One morning the power was interrupted – this was not unusual – and as a result production stopped.

Normally the power was restored within the hour but on this particular morning it stayed off. On contacting the supply company the managing director was informed that the substation had burnt out and it would be at least two days before restoration.

This caused the company a major problem. It had no power for its computers, phone system, fax, office or warehouse. It had no paper records as everything was computer-based and there was no backup. As a consequence the company could not access customer, staff or supplier records. Although it had products in the warehouse the staff did not know what was to be despatched where and could not access the warehouse, anyway, without lighting. Having sent the staff home the company could not then contact them about when to return to work. Meanwhile its customer had vast quantities of meat awaiting processing at its plant.

Lesson: always ensure you have access to key information that is not dependent upon a functioning computer system.

The company featured above has now installed a small generator to provide resilience.

Any incident that results in the invocation of incident management and business continuity arrangements will cause disruption to people, including the organization's staff, customers, contractors, partners and the community in general. The greater and longer the disruption, the greater the impact will be upon people. An organization has a duty of care and statutory/contractual requirements to protect people.

To achieve an effective recovery the organization should ensure that appropriate HR policies and procedures are developed as part of the overall recovery arrangements. The HR policies and procedures should cover two distinct areas:

1. managing people during the recovery phase; and
2. supporting people after the organization has recovered.

On invocation, it is important to ensure that the HR policies and procedures recognize and address the impact disruption will have on people affected by the incident. Failure to acknowledge and manage the issues can lead to resentment and demotivation, and hence a degradation in the organization's capability at the time when it is most vulnerable.

The effects on people of a major incident and subsequent disruption do not end at the point when the organization has fully recovered, albeit to a new normality. For many the effects will last for a considerable time. It is therefore essential that HR policies and procedures are put in place to respond to the needs of employees over an extended period.

BSI has published PD 25111, *Business continuity management – Guidance on human aspects of business continuity*, which provides detailed advice on managing people during and following a disruptive incident.

It is important for an organization to develop strategies to ensure supply chain continuity, as there are occasions where the organization relies on critical suppliers to deliver key products and services on time. ISO 22301 requires an organization to conduct evaluations of the business continuity capabilities of suppliers that are identified as critical during the BIA process.

As stated earlier, customers and clients expect the organization to take responsibility for its supply chains and are likely to hold the organization (rather than its suppliers) responsible for failure to deliver products or services. In addition the organization might be responsible under legislation for poor delivery, even if the issue lies within the supply chain. Therefore, the organization's reputation and brand is at risk of damage in the event of a problem in its supply chain or by the actions of a supplier.

BSI has published PD 25222, *Business continuity management – Guidance on supply chain continuity* that can be used to assess the effectiveness of suppliers' continuity. Major organizations are increasingly asking their key suppliers to comply with recognized BCM standards, in many cases requesting proof through the supplier obtaining certification.

It is recommended that four scenarios be considered when developing strategies. The cause that lies behind the scenario should not be considered. Instead it is the impact if it should occur that should be taken into account. The four scenarios are:

1.   denial of access to plant or premises;
2.   shortage of staff;
3.   failure of technology; and
4.   failure of a key supplier or partner.

There are three levels at which strategies can be set:

1.   full availability – cannot fail;
2.   recovery within RTO at an agreed minimum level (MBCO); and
3.   do nothing.

Full availability is provided where any disruption to the activity cannot be tolerated. Examples are 999 emergency call answering, e-banking activities or the A&E department in a hospital. Duplication of the activities and the resources that support them is the most appropriate way to achieve full availability. In the case of e-banking this may involve the provision of a second online computer facility at a separate site running in parallel with the primary site, served by a duplicated telecommunications network.

Where resumption of the activity can be phased over a period of time, it is possible to agree levels of resumption at fixed points in time. Consideration of the impact on the organization of the disruption over time will set the parameters for this approach, e.g. 25 per cent (minimum level agreed) to be available in two hours, 50 per cent in two days, full service in one week.

Examples of solutions that meet this approach are:

- standby offices equipped with PCs and telephones where staff delivering critical activities can be accommodated at short notice;
- alternative suppliers or the storage of buffer stocks;
- the use of interim managers to fill critical posts; and
- reciprocal arrangements with a similar organization.

If the strategy to be used is based on full availability or, alternatively, recovery within RTO at an agreed minimum level, then the type and amount of resources needed to achieve this have to be identified. Appendix L provides a basis for recording resource requirements while Appendix M sets out possible strategies that relate to the organization's key resources.

Doing nothing is an acceptable option. However, there are impacts that, if not managed, will subsequently have serious implications for the organization. These may be financial or, more likely, damage to reputation. In preparing the case for this option it is important to identify the range of impacts that will arise over time and establish appropriate actions to counteract them, e.g. communications to stakeholders as to why the decision to do nothing has been taken. An example of such a strategy would be a local authority suspending the processing of planning applications in the event of an emergency in the community.

Backlog trap

If the decision is to suspend or reduce the level of activity for a particular set of services or products, then arrangements must be made to 'catch up' by carrying out the outstanding work that has built up during the disruption. This may involve working overtime, outsourcing work or even deciding not to resume work at all. Some organizations that managed to weather a disruption have subsequently failed by not being able to overcome the backlog of work.

A small, regional broadband communications supplier was attracting many new customers as a result of its pricing policies. As more customers were signed up its system response slowed down. This resulted in a large number of customer complaints to the already stretched customer service staff. An upgrade to the system was initiated but this resulted in more complaints as problems arose with the installation.

New call centre staff were recruited but went live before being fully trained. The number of outstanding complaints escalated even further. At this point the media became involved. The company could no longer keep on top of complaints and the backlog built up to such an extent that customers began leaving. Eventually the company was forced to sell out to a national provider.

There will be cost implications for each strategy chosen. Wherever possible these must be set against the cost of disruption. It must be appreciated that in some cases the impact of financial cost cannot be applied to the activity. It may be that the greatest impact would be damage to reputation or embarrassment for elected representatives.

The decision on what levels of resilience and continuity are to be applied within the organization falls to the top management, which must sign off strategies to support the key products or services, as well as critical processes and activities and their supporting resources, acknowledging the cost implications, before any planning activities can commence.

Chapter 9 Establish and implement business continuity procedures

Incident response structure

The term 'incident' has been used in ISO 22301 but is frequently replaced with 'crisis' or 'emergency'. Every organization, regardless of size, must have a procedure in place to deal with a disruptive incident.

An incident response structure (IRS) supports all levels of activities that take place during a disruptive incident. If no structure exists there is a danger that response, continuity and eventual recovery plans will be operated independently of each other. This may cause delays, conflicts, incorrect allocation of resources and failure to achieve required levels of continuity.

It is critical that the organization moves at the speed of the incident in order to maintain control of the situation. In a larger organization it is strongly recommended that separation exists at the operational and tactical levels between teams that manage the emergency situation, e.g. fire and evacuation, and the teams responsible for ensuring continuity of operations. The mistake has been made in the public sector of having the same individuals trying to manage a public emergency situation, e.g. flooding, and also trying to manage their own authority's continuity. This has proved to be impractical and exhausting for the management team involved.

Procedures must be appropriate to the size and nature of the organization and set out the basis for determining when a disruption has occurred and how plans will be invoked. The timeline for response is shown in Figure 16. The diagram indicates a sequential implementation of incident, continuity and recovery plans. However, in some cases the plans may be implemented in rapid succession or simultaneously.

There are four elements within a good IRS:

1. situation assessment;
2. IRS activation;
3. communication capability; and
4. decision-making processes.

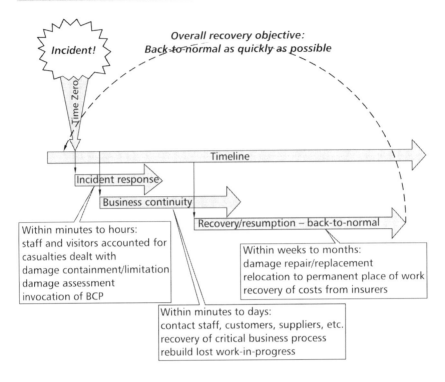

Figure 16 – Incident response timeline

Source: PD 25888:2011

1.   Assessment

The incident response procedure must identify the authority that determines the scale and severity of the disruption. There must be a process in place for undertaking an initial assessment of the situation, together with an ongoing process of monitoring and reporting to those who are managing the incident.

2.   Activation

The IRS must specify the process to be used to activate the plans, who should be consulted and informed. Authority for activation should be invested at the appropriate level. If the disruption is at business unit level, the local manager should have the authority to invoke the plan. Investing the authority for invocation at a high level might not be appropriate and could delay the response, causing the situation to get out of control and lead to serious consequences for the organization.

For six days in January 1998 freezing rain coated large parts of
Canada, resulting in 7–11 cm of ice being deposited on
telephone and power cables. The weight of the ice brought
down poles and transmission towers, causing massive power
and telephone outages that left four million people without
electricity supply, some for as long as a month. The authority to
invoke the power company's emergency plan was vested in the
senior executives who were still away at their holiday homes.
Contact could not be made with them as the landline
communications to their remote locations were lost. This
delayed the company's response to the emergency.

Lesson: ensure there is always someone on duty that has the
authority to invoke the plan.

3. Communication

If the plans are invoked it is essential that all interested parties are
informed and kept up to date. Who is to be informed and who will
manage communication must be established as part of the IRS. This
would include the media, if appropriate: a media spokesperson should be
nominated in the IRS. Clear and concise communication is required at the
time of disruption.

This activity has now been included as a requirement in ISO 22301 under
Clause 8.4.3 Warning and communication. It requires an organization to
'establish, implement and maintain procedures for

a) detecting an incident,
b) regular monitoring of an incident,
c) internal communication within the organization and receiving,
documenting and responding to communication from interested
parties,
d) receiving, documenting and responding to any national or regional
risk advisory system or equivalent,
e) assuring availability of the means of communication during a
disruptive incident,
f) facilitating structured communication with emergency responders,
g) recording of vital information about the incident, actions taken and
decisions made, and the following shall also be considered and
implemented where applicable:
   • alerting interested parties potentially impacted by an actual or
impending disruptive incident;
   • assuring the interoperability of multiple responding
organizations and personnel;
   • operation of a communications facility.

The communication and warning procedures shall be regularly exercised.'

4. Decision making

It is important that at the time of a major disruption the organization has in place a structure that will allow the management to make informed decisions and to take control of the situation. Organizations whose management style is normally based on debate and consensus will have to switch to a command and control structure (see Figure 17). The emergency services and the military have no problem with this approach, as it is their normal management style. Other organizations will have problems with this approach if the incident response team has not rehearsed before an incident occurs.

The model shown in Figure 17 is suitable for large- and medium-sized organizations. Small enterprises will have limited management resources to allocate to tactical and strategic responsibilities. In these circumstances it is essential that those who are managing the incident take time to address strategic and tactical issues, notwithstanding the pressing need to fix the problem at an operational level.

At the time of a major disruption it is possible that conflicting priorities will arise, as resources will be limited and all managers believe their areas of responsibility are critical. The decisions about priorities should have been made when the BCM strategies were developed and not at the time of the disruption. However, every situation is different and there must be a mechanism in place to adjust priorities accordingly. The strategic BCM team must be empowered to confirm or realign priorities as appropriate.

Incident response team

ISO 22301 requires an organization to establish 'procedures and a management structure to respond to a disruptive incident using personnel with the necessary responsibility, authority and competence to manage an incident'. The incident response team (IRT) should be assembled at a predetermined command centre and comprise people in positions who understand and represent the organization. One possible team structure is shown in Figure 18 below.

Team leader: the team leader is responsible for managing the IRT and is the primary contact with the appropriate company executives. The team leader is usually the person who decides, against predefined thresholds, that the incident should be handled by the IRT and assembles the team. The team leader ensures that all team functions are covered and initiates the plan to address the incident.

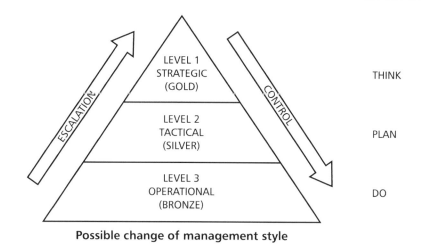

Possible change of management style

Figure 17 – Model of a command and control structure

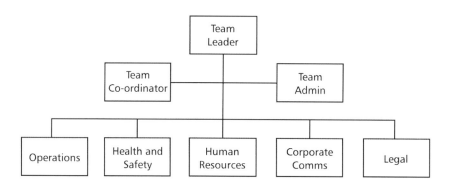

Figure 18 – Possible incident response team structure

Ideally, the team leader should be a strong senior executive or manager who is trusted and decisive, with a long-term perspective, and who should be freed from other responsibilities to lead the IRT until the incident is over or passed to the business continuity and recovery teams.

Health and safety: this person co-ordinates the health and safety response from the corporate level. They may also be responsible for environmental issues. The health and safety person provides the high-level contact for the 'blue light services' and government agencies, and provides advice on proper protective equipment and other health and safety matters. This person may also be responsible for advising the wider community of potential hazards from the incident, e.g. chemical discharge.

Corporate communications: this person ensures accurate and timely public response is being made together with appropriate press releases and contact with the media. They co-ordinate internal communications to executives, staff and other interested parties. This person ensures legal advice is taken when preparing communications. They advise the incident scene in media relations if required.

Human resources: this person ensures people issues are being addressed and co-ordinates these with the site's HR people. They provide for crisis counselling, access to the employee database, support in contacting family members, and assembling necessary internal and external HR resources if required.

Legal: this person provides legal counsel to the team and arranges for external legal support as needed. They participate in communication preparation and provide advice on securing the incident scene for subsequent investigation.

Operations: representatives from the organization's products and service delivery areas who provide advice and support as appropriate.

Team co-ordinator: this person or persons stays in the command centre and ensures the members are working with the most current information, and assists the team leader in managing the IRT activities including:

- recording information and comments from the team;
- making the team leader aware of new information;
- updating the IRT on any national or regional risks occurring;
- maintaining the incident log of actions taken and decisions made;
- updating team members as they arrive or return to the command centre;
- assisting the team leader in managing IRT activities; and
- documenting key phone numbers, contacts, etc. that may not have been recorded prior to the incident.

Team administration: if not a specific individual, these duties need to be assumed by one or more team members. The individual or individuals:

- helps to set up the incident command centre;
- ensures ICT equipment is ready to use;
- provides computer support to access data and procedures;
- operates and relays fax(es) and emails;
- provides copies of documents, e.g. Incident Response Plan;
- provides news updates and weather reports;

- gathers information that may be needed – e.g. external resources; and
- ensures welfare arrangements for the IRT are in place.

Deputies should be appointed to all positions for two reasons. First, this provides cover for team members' absence due to holidays, sickness, etc. and secondly, if the IRT has to operate over an extended period of time then it is advisable to rotate team members to avoid stress and tiredness.

When first assembled the team should decide on a schedule for meetings, typically every two or three hours depending on the nature of the incident. During the 'heat of the moment' all key issues are addressed. The meetings should last approximately 20–30 minutes, allowing time for the team members to action the decisions taken.

It is recommended that the incident control procedures include a standard agenda for the team leader to work to. A possible agenda might be:

1. reports on actions taken in previous period;
2. situation review and analysis;
3. decisions required in short term and long term;
4. decisions on activating business continuity arrangements;
5. allocation of tasks;
6. allocation of briefings, internally and externally;
7. briefing and directing of others; and
8. standing down.

Training

It is essential that all members, including deputies, are competent and can operate effectively as a team. Training needs must be assessed and provided; this will include appropriate training for any person who will be required to be interviewed by the media.

The team must undertake scenario-style exercises designed to familiarize it with the challenges incident management will present. Interested parties will be monitoring how well the disruptive incident is being managed and their confidence in the organization will be damaged if it is poorly handled. Good communications with the interested parties is critical to maintain confidence (see Communication above).

Command centre

The organization must establish an appropriate, prepared, location where the IRT will meet to manage the incident. This may be a room within the organization, if not a dedicated command centre, e.g. the boardroom or training room; it must be available when needed. Alternatively, the facility may be outside in a hotel or at a specialist provider. Experience has shown that it is advisable to have a secondary command centre available as the prime centre may be impacted by the incident or access denied by the 'blue light' services.

The centre may be equipped with, or have easy access to:

- telephones – fixed, mobile, satellite;
- fax machine;
- dedicated computer with internet and intranet access;
- data network connections;
- printer and photocopier;
- audio and/or video conferencing equipment;
- TV with satellite connection – provides ability to monitor the news;
- key office supplies – pens, markers, flip charts, paper, etc.;
- LED projector and screen;
- status board;
- clock(s) – multiple if more than one time zone is involved;
- sign in/out board – to track location of team members;
- hard copy backups of incident management plans, business continuity plans, employee records, contact lists and key site or reference information; and
- welfare arrangements for incident team members.

Chapter 10   Incident response and business continuity plans

The first action for many organizations in establishing BCM has been to create a business continuity plan without going through the key steps outlined in the previous chapters. The danger in taking this approach is that it will not result in a true understanding of the organization and how it delivers key products or services. Consideration of various strategies and their resource requirements may have been missed. As a result the plan produced may not be fit for purpose and may not offer the protection and benefits that would have been possible. By completing the processes set out earlier the organization can now develop realistic and appropriate business continuity plans.

Experience has shown that organizations can be disrupted for many reasons. Business continuity planning has traditionally been based on known threats: loss of IT, loss of a building through fire, flooding, etc. In recent times, however, the UK has experienced some unexpected disruptions, including a widespread outbreak of foot-and-mouth disease, extensive disruptions to the rail network, a national shortage of oil-based fuels, the loss of water supplies for weeks and a volcanic ash cloud. In most cases existing plans did not cover these disruptions and the impacts they had on the day-to-day operations of organizations.

When developing plans it is important that all elements of the organization are involved (see Figure 19). If this does not happen assumptions may be made about the ability of other parts of the organization to respond and meet the needs of the plan. For example if the plan calls for members of staff to work from home then the IT department must confirm that technical arrangements have or can be made to enable this to happen. The HR department may need to adjust its policies to accommodate remote working and health and safety policies may have to be modified.

Incident and continuity plans are used under challenging and stressful circumstances; they should be concise, simple and easy to follow. In addition plans should ensure the organization maintains compliance with applicable laws and regulations during the period of their implementation.

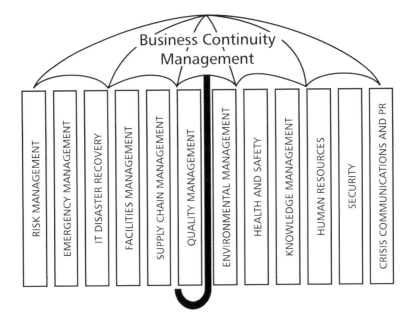

Figure 19 – Involving everyone in the planning process

Plans should provide answers to the basic questions:

- What is to be done?
- When?
- Where are the alternative resources located?
- Who is involved?
- How is continuity to be achieved?

In any organization there may be a suite of interconnected plans covering emergency, business continuity, incident management and recovery management. The plans produced should be appropriate for the organization.

A small organization, operating from one site, may only need a single document that covers incident management and continuity management, while larger organizations will need integrated corporate, divisional and business unit plans based on a common structure. These in turn may be underpinned by action plans for front-line operations, e.g. hospital wards (see Figure 20). Such plans must be synchronized to eliminate conflicts and ensure that agreed restoration priorities are achieved. In a large organization a central BCM team or BCM co-ordinator undertakes this role.

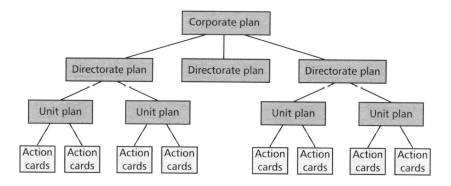

Figure 20 – Corporate business continuity plan structure

The organization will need to create plans that detail how it will achieve continuity of operations (business continuity plans) that are based on the previously agreed timescales and minimum levels for the activities that support the key products and services.

Many large organizations have functional departments that deliver support services across many business units, e.g. ICT, HR, facilities and finance. Support departments should develop BCM plans that meet the needs of the business units to continue the operation of critical processes and activities. The RTOs and, in the case of ICT, the recovery point objectives (RPOs) must be driven by the business requirement not the capabilities of the functional department. If the department cannot meet the required RTOs, e.g. ICT recovering network services, then the business unit may need to include alternative arrangements until the support service is resumed.

Plans will be subject to change and therefore version control and configuration management must be applied. Each copy of the plan must be numbered and subject to controlled distribution. Where sensitive information is contained in plans they must be given the appropriate level of confidentiality.

Plans may take various formats. They may be written as text or flow charts, or be produced by specialist software. They can be held on the company intranet or secure areas of the internet, or be paper-based, held on a personal digital assistant (PDA), a tablet computer or in a simple 'wallet' format. Plans should not be vast documents as they will have to be used in times of stress and therefore should be kept as straightforward as possible, containing the minimum amount of information to enable the team to deliver continuity. They must be accessible at all times to those named individuals who are required to use them.

On several occasions when major incidents have occurred in London the police have been forced to evacuate and cordon off large areas of commercial districts. Individuals were found trying to cross the cordon lines to get access to their building. When challenged they informed the authorities that they needed to get their business continuity plan as it had been left in the office.

Lesson: make certain there are copies of incident and continuity plans available at all times and that additional copies are kept off site.

Within a large organization a common template may be used for the creation of incident and continuity plans. There are frequent requests from organizations for standard templates to be published that just require 'box filling'. While such a template would be useful as a guideline, it must be recognized that no two organizations are the same and even separate locations within the same organization will have differences. The plan must therefore reflect the organization rather than the organization being made to fit a standard template.

For many organizations the threat of a global flu pandemic has driven the requirement to develop business continuity. Plans are written for that unique scenario, which included specific arrangements covering occupational health, HR policies and security. While these are important areas to be addressed if a flu pandemic should occur, these elements of a business continuity plan should be owned by the specific functions that are responsible for maintaining the content. Good practice ensures that these elements are documented separately and the business continuity plans signpost where the documents are located, e.g. by hyperlinks within an electronic plan. This ensures that the latest arrangements are available and minimizes the workload of the business continuity plan owner.

Ownership of the plan must be identified. In larger organizations there will be plans at different levels. Business unit managers should own operational plans. All plans must be reviewed regularly and also when significant changes occur to the organization or the environment in which it operates. The responsible owner must undertake the review that is then signed off at a higher level. An example of a plan review is contained in Appendix N.

The plans must also take account of any external arrangements for managing an incident. These include the actions of the emergency services, local authorities and other external agencies in the event of a major disruption and, if sharing a building, the contingency arrangements of the facilities management company or landlord.

Plan contents

The following sections discuss the recommended elements of incident response and business continuity plans.

Purpose and scope: should be clearly defined.

Objectives: details of the priority order for continuity and recovery of key products or services and their critical activities must be available together with their RTOs and recovery levels (MBCOs).

Assumptions and dependencies: the plan should indicate what assumptions have been applied, e.g. worst-case scenario: ICT facilities will not be available for five days. It should also indicate any interdependencies and interactions that are necessary for the plan to work.

Roles and responsibilities: the plan should identify the roles and responsibilities of those post holders who will be involved in delivering the plan. It will identify the team leader, key team members and their deputies to be assembled at the time of invocation. It will set out their levels of authority (including financial authority) and to whom they must report their actions. It will also set out the point at which the responsibility for incident or continuity management must pass to a higher level in the organization. There may be separate teams responsible for incident and continuity plans.

Invoking the plan: the plan must indicate the circumstances under which it is to be invoked and who can authorize the invocation. It must also include details of how to manage a disruption and its impact upon the organization. It is essential that an organization responds quickly if a crisis or disaster is to be avoided. The invocation of a business unit plan may need a lower level of authority to deal with a local incident. It is important that any invocation is flagged to senior management so it is aware that an incident exists and can consider the wider implications for the organization. Instructions to that effect should be written into the plan.

Command centre: details of the main and secondary locations where the team should proceed to in order to manage the disruption.

Alternative locations: details of standby locations should be included, together with maps, security arrangements to gain access, contractual terms and any other relevant information.

System recovery plans: small companies may include basic system recovery plans within the main document. These may consist of instructions on how to restore data or transfer telecommunications services to an alternative location. In larger organizations the recovery plans will be complex and may be separate documents owned by the unit responsible for providing the service, e.g. IT recovery plans for a major data centre. The main plan should identify the recovery plan owners and the key actions they will take.

Contact details: the plan should include contact details of the IRT members and their deputies. In addition it may include other details for internal and external contacts as follows:

- key senior management;
- key operational staff;
- emergency services;
- local authority officers;
- regulators and other compliance bodies;
- suppliers;
- key customers/clients;
- utility companies;
- insurers; and
- media organizations.

It may be appropriate to include details of contracts, insurance policies, regulatory requirements, etc. These additional documents may be stored separately to the plan itself but should be accessible.

Vital documents and resources: a list of vital documents and resources needed for continuity and recovery for each critical activity must be included along with details of where these are located. These should be based on the output from the BIA. Vital documents may include records of who is authorized to retrieve materials as well as security arrangements, e.g. passwords that will be required. Vital materials may include stationery, spare parts, specialist machinery and tools.

Checklists: a simple checklist or action card may be included to ensure the team completes mandatory tasks. Meeting agendas can be included so that all key elements of the process are covered when the team meets. (See Chapter 9.)

Incident log: with any major disruption there may be a requirement for post-event inquiry and audit. It is vital therefore that a record is maintained of what actions were taken, why they were taken, when they were taken and who took them. An example of an incident log is shown in Appendix O.

People issues: special consideration must be given to the needs of staff, contractors and visitors who may have been evacuated from the normal premises without time to collect their personal belongings, e.g. money, credit cards, keys and identity cards. There may be injuries or deaths and immediate family would have to be informed. The organization has a duty of care to its staff and these personnel issues will need to be addressed as part of the incident plan, which must identify whose responsibility it is to deal with the people issues.

Plans must also take account of the welfare of those who will be managing the disruption, comply with health and safety requirements and ensure there are sufficient team members available to work shifts in the event of the disruption extending over a long period.

Communications: details of what will be communicated, and to whom, must be included together with details of those who are responsible for delivery of the messages. This will cover internal and external communications. Larger organizations may choose to have a separate incident communication plan to cover this area.

Salvage: this is an area frequently omitted from BCM. If the organization has suffered fire, flooding or other damage to its buildings then it is important to ensure that, when safe to do so, arrangements are made to recover important documents and equipment. Documents and equipment that are damaged by water or other contaminants can be cleaned and restored by specialist contractors. As time is of the essence it will assist with recovery if there are pre-existing arrangements in place with appropriate contractors to carry out such restoration work.

Returning to normal: a process must exist for standing down the incident and continuity teams and returning to normal once the disruption is over.

The nature, complexity and scale of recovery cannot fully be determined in advance of an incident; therefore, the management of the recovery has to be flexible, scalable and relevant to a broad range of risks applicable to the organization and its operating environment.

Some incidents are dramatic and could change the very fabric of 'normality' for the organization and its stakeholders, so lessons have to be learned from the response to any incident and any pre-planned recovery arrangements reviewed. For this reason, the organization may need to function under new operating norms beyond recovering to pre-recovery conditions.

It is necessary that an organization's recovery arrangements interface with any incident management and BCM arrangements.

BSI has published PD 25888, *Business continuity management – Guidance on organization recovery following disruptive incidents*, which provides comprehensive guidance on organization recovery following damaging incidents.

Implementation

Having completed the plans, they must be implemented. Those who hold positions that are named in the plan must be made aware of their role and have the appropriate training to enable them to fulfil their responsibilities. The section on training in Chapter 6, including the key steps for establishing a training programme, provide useful guidance on training. Exercising plans is one of the principal methods of ensuring that those who will be involved in managing an incident and implementing continuity are aware of the contents of the plan and their roles. Exercising is covered in Chapter 11.

Interested parties, both internal and external, need to be aware that the organization has plans in place to deal with disruptions. They need to be conscious of what will be done, what products and services will be available, and at what levels. Where appropriate, they will also need to know what activities the organization will not be doing while it recovers.

External stakeholders, partners and suppliers that have a role to play in assisting the organization to cope with disruption need to know their role and responsibilities in supporting the organization's requirements. As these partners and suppliers may also be affected by the same disruption it is important that they have plans to maintain their own continuity of service.

Appendix P shows an example of a possible plan structure. It is important to note that plans must be appropriate to the organization and support the management of a disruptive incident, not hinder it. A simple action card might be appropriate at the business unit level to commence the incident response, with the full plans being held at the command centre locations.

Chapter 11   Exercising and testing

BCM requires that effective plans be established to ensure an organization can respond to any incident. But the process does not stop at the planning stage.

ISO 22301 requires the organization to have exercised and tested its business continuity procedures to ensure they are consistent with its business continuity scope and objectives.

Plans are worthless unless they are exercised. Many examples exist where organizations have had business continuity plans in place but the plans failed because they had not been exercised. In the UK, research has shown (Chartered Management Institute, 2012) that only half of those organizations with plans exercise or test them at least on an annual basis while 18 per cent never exercise their plans at all (see Figure 21).

The exercising of plans is essential as it is highly unlikely that any plan created will work first time. Exercising ensures that disconnections and omissions within the plan are fixed before it is used in reality. Seventy-six per cent of those organizations that carried out exercises found errors in their plans. It is far better to have found the errors when the plan was exercised rather than the first time it is invoked in response to a real incident. Having found the errors it is essential that time-specified actions are created to rectify the errors and omissions. Figure 22 shows the latest results of rehearsals for UK organizations.

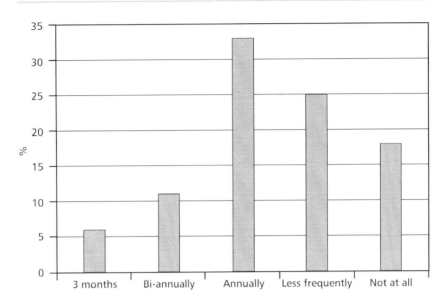

Figure 21 – Frequency with which UK organizations exercise business continuity plans

Source: Chartered Management Institute, 2012

Did rehearsals reveal shortcomings?

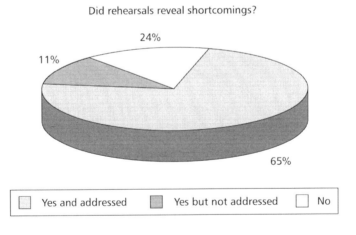

Figure 22 – Results of BCM rehearsals

Source: Chartered Management Institute, 2012

Exercising helps to build confidence in team members by clarifying roles and responsibilities, and supplying practical training and awareness, as well as providing valuable experience of responding to an incident.

There are various forms of exercise but it is important to:

* test the systems;
* exercise the plans; and
* rehearse the people.

Examples of tests for systems may be to ensure that the standby generator starts when power is interrupted, that the telephone divert arrangements work or that data can be recovered from the backup source.

> The managing director of a small company that relied on IT systems ensured that a backup of important data was taken every day, copied onto a tape. He took the tape home every night, placing it in the side pocket of his car door.
>
> When a problem occurred with the company's IT server, attempts were made to use the backup tape to recover the data only to find the tape was blank. By placing the tape in the door pocket it had been adjacent to one of the car's loudspeakers and the magnetic field generated by the loudspeaker had wiped the data from the tape.
>
> Lesson: tapes should be stored in a safe, off-site environment, there should be more than one copy and regular data restore tests should be undertaken.

Testing should ensure that technical systems work correctly and that operating instructions are clear and valid for the equipment. The tests should be as close to live working as possible, e.g. full load being taken by the generator. Another form of test that should be carried out on a regular basis is a 'call cascade'. This is used to verify lines of communication that will be used when invoking the plans.

Plans should be exercised to ensure they are comprehensive and realistic. The first exercise should be one to 'prove the plan works' and should be sold as a learning exercise. Prior to this first exercise it is advisable for the plan to be read by someone who has not been involved in producing the document. This is to ensure the plan is clear and makes sense to others, to check that it takes account of all the people involved and to spot any gaps in the document.

Exercising is not about achieving a pass or a fail but ensuring the plan works as intended. It is also a training opportunity for those who are named in the documents. There are certain key rules to be observed when planning exercises.

Exercises must have defined aims and objectives that may include:

- affirmation that everyone understands their role and that there is an overall appreciation of the plan;
- checking that invocation procedures/call-out communications work;
- ensuring that the accommodation, equipment, systems and services provided are appropriate and operational; and
- verifying that the critical activities that support key products or services can be recovered within their RTOs and to the levels (MBCOs) required.

BSI has published PD 25666, *Business continuity management – Guidance on exercising and testing for continuity and contingency programmes*, which provides comprehensive guidance.

Exercises should not 'risk' the organization by causing disruptions. They must be practical and cost-effective, appropriate to the organization and designed to build confidence in the plans.

> A very large public sector organization was testing the uninterruptible power supply (UPS) that served its main computer systems. A failure occurred with the UPS that caused the mains power to the computers to trip out, resulting in a complete loss of systems. In the rush to restore power, the trip switch was restored but this caused a massive spike in voltage to the computers. This burned out several key components in the computers. Alternative systems were established but full restoration took several weeks. It was acknowledged that the test had not been properly planned and no risk assessment had been undertaken.
>
> Lesson: planning your exercise and carrying out impact and risk assessments is very important.

A regular programme of exercises should be established and documented. These should take place at a period determined by top management or when there have been significant changes to the organization or the environment in which it operates. ISO 22301 requires top management to be actively involved in exercising and testing as a demonstration of the commitment to the BCMS.

Observers should be appointed to note the way the incident and continuity teams handle the situation. Every effort must be made to gain full participation from those involved. If the organization has an internal audit function there is value in inviting someone from this department to attend and provide feedback on performance against the plan.

There are various forms of exercise ranging from desktop review, where the participants review and challenge the contents of the plan, a 'walk-through' where the interaction between players is assessed, to a full plan test where the site or building is shut down and a move undertaken to an alternative location. Full plan testing is the only way to assure all concerned parties that the incident and continuity management arrangements will work when required. Appendix Q shows the relationship between the various types of exercises.

To exercise a plan the BCM management should decide upon an appropriate scenario that has relevance to the organization. Initially it may be appropriate to exercise elements of the plan separately, resolving any gaps found, before running a complete plan exercise. It is important that the scenario is changed each time the exercise is performed in order to challenge the plan and ensure all its components are examined.

Full plan testing is not always appropriate so the organization must ensure that an exercise programme is constructed that, taken together over time, validates the whole of the business continuity arrangement and involves relevant parties.

As disruptions occur without warning there is benefit in running a snap exercise where only the minimum number of people are made aware that the exercise is to take place.

An exercise can be run in real time or compressed time so that a plan can be exercised in one session. It is important to include timeout periods so that people and teams can clarify their understanding of the exercise. Because the exercise will require intense concentration from the players, careful consideration should be given to the length of time taken by the exercise and the players' welfare arrangements.

Rehearsing the team players is vital. People demonstrate different characteristics when put under pressure. A real invocation will be a stressful situation and it is important to understand the strengths and weaknesses of the individuals concerned. As previously stated, in the UK the normal management culture surrounding decision making is based on consensus with the maximum information being available to all parties. At times of plan invocation the management style may have to move to command and control, working with less than perfect information.

Different leadership styles are needed and it could be that the initial teams chosen lack certain skills. Some of these can be acquired through training but often it will be necessary to change roles or even exclude people from the team. It is not always the most senior person who is best at managing a disruptive incident.

A log of all actions and outcomes must be made during the exercise and this must be reviewed as soon as possible after the event. It is a good idea for this review to be carried out with the participants so they can express their own views on what went well or otherwise.

To assist with this, participants should be asked to maintain their own diary of events throughout the exercise. The views of the independent observers should also be included.

A post-exercise report should be completed that includes recommendations on actions to adjust the plans. A senior manager of the unit in which the exercise was conducted should sign off the report and the actions to be taken. The process of exercising is set out in Figure 23.

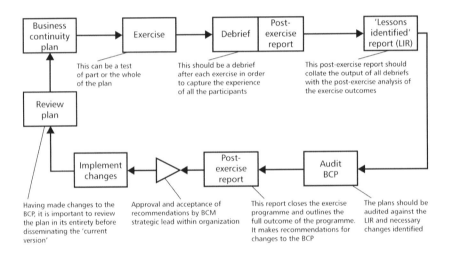

Figure 23 – The exercising cycle

Source: HM Government, 2005

Documentation from the exercise programme provides clear evidence to auditors that BCM is being taken seriously within the organization and as such would form a vital part of any documentation being submitted when seeking compliance with or certification to ISO 22301.

Chapter 12   Performance evaluation

This chapter relates to the Check element of the BCMS and covers monitoring and reviewing of the BCMS and business continuity performance. It is essential that the organization conduct evaluations at planned internals or when significant changes occur.

Maintaining the BCMS

Nothing stands still; organizations are in a continual state of flux. Staff change; some will leave and new people will join. Roles and responsibilities can alter, especially at a time of reorganization. Mergers, acquisitions, organic growth and downsizing mean that structures and reporting lines will evolve. Suppliers and customers change, and regulatory and legal environments may be adjusted; political conditions in supply countries may become unstable. An outsourcing contract may change the responsibility for critical functions, e.g. IT being outsourced to a third party. New products and services may be introduced, or new sites opened or others closed. At the basic level, contact details will always be changing.

It is therefore essential that the BCMS and the BCM arrangements be subject to regular monitoring, measurement and review.

Processes must be established whereby any change that will affect business continuity arrangements is flagged up to the BCM manager. This includes the changes in any other policies that could have an impact on BCM, e.g. risk management. Adjustments to the BCMS and business continuity plans should be made if the changes are minor. If major changes have occurred it may be necessary to revisit the BIA to reassess critical activities. New continuity strategies may be required and the incident and continuity plans changed. Any changes made to the BCMS and the BCM arrangements must be subject to the appropriate levels of sign-off.

Regardless of whether there have been changes or not, the BCM arrangements should be subject to an annual review to ensure they are still current. Senior management should review the list of key products or services and an assessment should be made about the criticality of supporting activities and their priority for recovery. Checks should be made to ensure that the supporting resources and interdependencies are still correct. Plans should be reviewed to ensure they are still appropriate and workable. An appropriate management level should sign off the reviews regardless of whether changes have or have not been made.

Staff will need to be made aware of any changes that have been made to the BCMS or BCM arrangements. The maintenance of document control is critical; it is important that version control is applied to BCM documentation and that a mechanism exists whereby updates are issued and old versions withdrawn.

With regard to the BCMS, ISO 22301 requires the organization to determine:

- 'what needs to be monitored and measured';
- establish valid methods for measurement and monitoring;
- determine how analysis and evaluation of the findings will be undertaken; and
- set a timetable for measurement, monitoring, analysis and evaluation.

Both quantitative and qualitative measures should be used to assure the organization that the BCMS is fit for purpose and is being correctly implemented and maintained.

One way this can be done is by the setting of key performance indicators (KPIs). These are normally numerical and quantity based and objectively assessed against targets. Examples are:

- the percentage of key products and services covered by the BCMS;
- the percentage of plans completed by a specified date;
- the number of awareness sessions completed by a specified date;
- the percentage of staff who have attended awareness sessions;
- the number of plans to be exercised, and types of exercise to be carried out, by a specified date;
- the percentage of actions resulting from the exercises that were completed within a specified timescale;
- the percentage of plans reviewed by the target date;
- the number of disruptive incidents or near misses experienced in a given period.

To evaluate the quality and effectiveness of the BCMS requires a different type of assessment that is more subjective. This can be undertaken by assessing elements of the BCMS against the organization's internal standards, industry good practice or the requirements of ISO 22301. Assessments may include:

- compliance with the organization's business continuity policies and objectives;
- compliance with applicable legal and regulatory requirements;

- the quality of the impact and risk analyses, and business continuity plans;
- the quality, breadth and clarity of exercise scripts and training materials;
- assessment of effectiveness of awareness and training of staff in relation to the BCMS and business continuity arrangements;
- the type of lessons identified from exercises;
- the level of impact caused by disruptive incidents;
- the effectiveness of the BCM arrangements when invoked;
- the lessons identified as a result of the post-incident reviews (see below);
- the stakeholders' awareness and satisfaction with the organization's BCM arrangements.

It is possible to use maturity models to measure the penetration and acceptance of BCM within an organization. These can be used to assess the current status of an existing BCMS and then be used on an annual basis to demonstrate improvement, or otherwise.

Some organizations use self-assessment questionnaires to determine the compliance with the BCM procedures and any standard adopted. A self-assessment checklist is included in Appendix R.

The organization must take action to address adverse trends or results emerging from evaluation activities. The output can be used to establish corrective actions and to set BCM objectives for the next 12 months.

The organization must retain documented evidence of the monitoring, measuring, analysis and evaluations that will facilitate corrective actions as appropriate.

Post-incident review

If the organization has suffered a disruptive incident that has resulted in the incident and/or continuity plans being invoked, arrangements should be in place to carry out a post-incident review to:

- establish the nature and cause of the incident;
- assess the adequacy of the management's response;
- assess the effectiveness of the plans to meet the RTOs and MBCOs;
- assess the capabilities of those involved in implementing the plans;
- identify any improvement that can be made to the BCMS and the business continuity arrangements; and
- establish a timetable for corrective actions to be taken.

Internal audit

The decision to introduce BCM into an organization will be taken at the highest level. The Chartered Management Institute's 2012 BCM awareness survey shows that the need for good corporate governance continues to provide the biggest reason why BCM is introduced into an organization. Top management needs to be assured that the BCMS and the BCM procedures are fit for purpose and are being correctly implemented.

Internal auditing involves measuring compliance with the organization's policies and procedures and provides value to governing bodies and top management as an objective source of independent advice. It provides a catalyst for improving an organization's effectiveness and efficiency by providing insight and recommendations based on analyses and assessments of the business continuity processes. If the organization has decided that it will comply with an appropriate standard, e.g. ISO 22301 (as quoted below), internal auditing also provides assurance that the BCMS and BCM comply with the standard.

The organization must:

- 'plan, establish, implement and maintain (an) audit programme(s), including the frequency, methods, responsibilities, planning requirements and reporting. The audit programme(s) shall take into consideration the importance of the processes concerned and the results of previous audits,
- define the audit criteria and scope for each audit';
- select competent auditors with a knowledge of BCM. Auditors may be internal or outsourced;
- conduct audits to ensure objectivity and the impartiality of the audit process;
- 'ensure that the results of the audits are reported to relevant management, and
- retain documented information as evidence of the implementation of the audit programme and the audit results.'

The management responsible for the area being audited shall ensure that any necessary corrections and corrective actions are taken without undue delay to eliminate detected nonconformities and their causes. Follow-up activities must verify the actions taken and the results recorded.

Management review

An important element of performance evaluation is the management review. Top management must review the organization's BCMS, at planned intervals, to ensure its continued suitability, adequacy and effectiveness.

The review must look for opportunities to improve or, if appropriate, change the structure of the BCMS. Areas to be covered include those set out in Chapters 3 to 6, with specific attention being given to the BCM policy and objectives for the organization. Consideration must be given to any changes in external or internal issues that are relevant to the BCMS. The output of the reviews, including identified 'opportunities for continual improvement', must be documented and records maintained.

Various sources of information can be used to inform the review. These include:

- output from BCMS audits and internal reviews;
- output from reviews of supplier and partner BCM arrangements;
- feedback from interested parties and recommendations for improvements;
- the status of nonconformities and corrective actions, including follow-up actions previously identified;
- the level of residual risk and changes in the organization's risk appetite;
- emerging vulnerabilities/threats and those not previously addressed adequately;
- output from exercises, including the lessons identified reports;
- observations/recommendations from incidents or near misses experienced by the organization and others;
- results of the education and awareness programmes;
- 'monitoring and measurement evaluation results';
- 'the status of actions from previous management reviews'; and
- developments in BCM techniques, products, procedures and good practice.

In developing the output of the review top management must take into consideration any changes to:

- the business;
- the risk appetite;
- risk and security requirements;
- operational conditions and processes;
- legal, regulatory and contractual requirements; and
- resource and budgetary requirements.

The output from the management review will include decisions and a timetable for the actions related to opportunities to continually improve the BCMS and the possible need for any changes to the system. These may include:

- 'variations to the scope of the BCMS;
- improvement of the effectiveness of the BCMS;
- update of the risk assessment, business impact analysis, business continuity plans and related procedures'; and

- how the effectiveness of the BCMS and BCM are measured.

The organization must retain documented evidence of the results of the management review. The results should be communicated to the relevant interested parties.

Chapter 13 Improvement

The final element of the PDCA cycle is Act, which requires the organization to identify and act on BCMS nonconformities through corrective actions. One of the key elements of a good management system is that it has the capacity for continual improvement. This is a key element of Deming's approach to quality management and it is also a requirement of ISO 22301. Continual improvement is based on the Japanese philosophy of *Kaizen*, which means 'change for the better' or 'improvement'.

The concept of *Kaizen* is easy to understand. However, it is often difficult to achieve on an ongoing basis in an organization due to complacency, distractions, loss of focus, lack of commitment, reassigned priorities and lack of resources. Chapter 5 referred to the risks and opportunities that surround the introduction of the BCMS and the need to develop appropriate action plans to deal with the risks if they should arise. An organization that fosters a climate of continual improvement will have greater success in maintaining a 'fit for purpose' BCMS.

> Tatung of Taiwan ran a television manufacturing facility in the UK. If any employee on the production line found a problem with quality, component shortage or production methods they were authorized to stop the line. Providing the problem was genuine, the employee was not blamed for loss of production but praised for possibly preventing faulty products from being produced.

Those working within, or who are closely associated with, an organization are an excellent source of suggestions for improvements. They can see areas where corrections can be made to systems and preventative measures can be built in to increase overall resilience. More often than not, however, the climate within the organization is such that they are reluctant to bring their suggestions to management.

Organizations need to encourage a process whereby individuals feel able to highlight omissions, duplications and failings without being rebutted or blamed in any way. It is those who work at the coalface who frequently know the solutions but the culture of the organization may prevent their ideas from surfacing. By using a suggestions scheme or discussing how BCM and the organization's resilience can be strengthened at team meetings and on a one-to-one basis, managers will be able to create a climate where continual improvement is the norm.

There are two actions associated with the final element of the BCMS: nonconformities and continuous improvement.

Nonconformity and corrective action

This is where the organization eliminates the cause of nonconformities associated with the BCMS in order to prevent their recurrence. ISO 22301 sets out the documented procedures for corrective actions:

'The organization shall

a) identify the nonconformity,
b) react to the nonconformity, and, as applicable,
    1) take action to control, contain and correct it, and
    2) deal with the consequences.'

ISO 22301 goes on to state that the organization shall also 'evaluate the need for action to eliminate the causes of the nonconformity, by

- reviewing the nonconformity,
- determining the causes of the nonconformity, in order that it does not recur or occur elsewhere, by …
- determining if similar nonconformities exist, or could potentially occur,
- evaluating the need for corrective action to ensure that nonconformities do not recur or occur elsewhere,
- determining and implementing corrective action needed,
- reviewing the effectiveness of any corrective action taken and
- making changes to the BCMS, if necessary.'

The organization must retain:

- 'the nature of the nonconformities and any subsequent actions taken, and
- the results of any corrective action' taken.

Continual improvement

Like any management system BCMS must be subject to continual improvement. The organization must make arrangements to ensure that it continually improves the suitability, adequacy and effectiveness of the BCMS through:

- the review of the business continuity policy and objectives;
- audit results;
- analysis of monitored events;
- corrective and preventative actions; and
- management review.

Chapter 14   Conclusion

Despite the increased use of BCM in organizations, there are still managers who continue to dismiss the need for continuity management even in the face of such major disruptions as the 2007 floods and 2010/2011 bad winters in the UK. Many have a strong belief that insurance will provide cover for any loss that they may suffer. This is not the case as losses are not restricted to material damage but also include loss of reputation, revenues and customers. Recommencement of operations after a disaster often takes far longer than anticipated, adding to the cost burden on the organization. As a result, the gap between the real cost of disasters and insurance payments is considerable.

Organizations can be disrupted in many ways. Incidents include fire, flood, water shortages, storm damage, internal and external vandalism or fraud, the failure of systems and loss of data, computer hacking, machinery breakdown, breaches of physical and system securities, and staff losses. These are only some examples. Added to this is the climate in which today's organization has to operate. The intolerance of customers and clients to failure, their lack of loyalty and the demands of the banks for financial viability add considerable pressure at a time of disruption. If the organization is unable to manage a disruption correctly and in good time then the situation will rapidly turn into a crisis and then a disaster, and the organization may fail. Small- and medium-sized enterprises are at greatest risk yet they are the first to ignore the benefits of BCM. As they form the foundation on which most economies operate, it is essential that they are encouraged to adopt BCM.

As recent disasters around the world have demonstrated, it is not possible to predict all possible events that can seriously disrupt an organization's ability to maintain continuity of operations. Because the unexpected will always occur, there is a clear need to protect organizations by forward planning. BCM is seen as a vital tool to achieve this. The new international BCM standard, ISO 22301:2012, built upon BS 25999-2, has been developed to enable organizations to demonstrate their capability through alignment or certification. This book sets out to help any organization, regardless of sector or size, to meet the requirements of ISO 22301. It does not claim to be a definitive guide but rather a route map that leads to the implementation of an effective BCMS.

Appendix A   BCM drivers by company sector

Sector	Principal drivers	Comments
Business services	Insurers, customers and corporate governance	Insurers are keen to reduce business interruption risks. Major customers demanding BCM.
Central government	Corporate governance	While not covered directly by legislation it is recognized that the continuity of government departments and agencies is critical.
Construction	Insurers, customers and corporate governance	Major contracts are driven by project management and penalty clauses. Health and safety issues are important – insurers look for good management.
Education	Corporate governance, regulators and central government	Funding bodies and auditors look for evidence of BCM.
Finance and insurance	Regulators, auditors and corporate governance	Industry is highly regulated and subject to a variety of audits.
Health and social care	Central government, legislation, regulation and corporate governance	Health services are a principal focus for government. The UK Civil Contingencies Act 2004 covers public bodies. The Care Quality Commission

Sector	Principal drivers	Comments
		and Monitor are the regulators.
IT and telecommunications	Insurers, customers and corporate governance	IT and telecommunications provide the underpinning infrastructure for most organizations. Telecommunications is a key element of the critical national infrastructure.
Local government and emergency services	Central government, legislation, auditors and corporate governance	These organizations are now subject to legislation under the Civil Contingencies Act 2004.
Manufacturing and production	Insurers, customers and corporate governance	Major customers have become aware of their supply chain vulnerabilities while insurers are keen to reduce business interruption risks.
Retail/wholesale	Insurers and customers	Retail outlets drive the wholesalers but the outlets themselves have many customers who individually have no voice.
Transport and logistics	Customers, regulators, insurers and corporate governance	Major players in supply chain logistics.
Utilities – electricity, gas, water	Regulators, insurers, auditors, customers and corporate governance	Critical infrastructure operated and maintained by regulated companies that have major customers. Subject to a variety of audits.

Appendix B   Cross references between BS 25999-2 and ISO 22301

BS 25999-2:2007	ISO 22301:2012	
	Directly related	**Does not cross-reference**
Introduction	0.1 General 0.2 The Plan-Do-Check-Act (PDCA) model	
1 Scope	1 Scope	
2 Terms and definitions		3 Terms and definitions, some terms omitted, new terms added, some redefined.
3.1 Planning the business continuity management system		4.1 Understanding of the organization and its context 6.1 Actions to address risks and opportunities (to the BCMS)
3.2.1 Scope and objectives of the BCMS	4.2 Understanding the needs and expectations of interested parties 4.3 Determining the scope of the management system 6.2 Business continuity objectives and plans to achieve them	
3.2.2 BCM policy	5.1 General	

BS 25999-2:2007	ISO 22301:2012	
	Directly related	**Does not cross-reference**
	5.2 Management commitment 5.3 Policy	
3.2.3 Provision of resources	7.1 Resources 5.2 Management commitment 5.4 Organizational roles, responsibilities and authorities 8.3.2 Establishing resource requirements	
3.2.4 Competency of BCM personnel	7.2 Competence	
3.3 Embedding BCM in the organization's culture	7.3 Awareness 7.4 Communication	
3.4 BCMS documentation and records	7.5 Documented Information 8.1 c) Operational planning and control	
4.1.1 Business impact analysis	8.2.1 General 8.2.2 Business impact analysis	
4.1.2 Risk assessment	8.2.1 General 8.2.3 Risk assessment	
4.1.3 Determining choices	8.3.3 Protection and mitigation	
4.2 Determining business continuity strategy	8.3.1 Determination and selection 8.3.2 Establishing resource requirements	
4.3.2 Incident response structure	8.4.2 Incident response structure	

BS 25999-2:2007	ISO 22301:2012	
	Directly related	**Does not cross-reference**
		8.4.3 Warning and communication
4.3.3 Business continuity plans and incident management plans	8.4.4 Business continuity plans	
		8.4.5 Recovery
4.4.2 BCM exercising	8.5 Exercising and testing	
4.4.3 Maintaining and reviewing BCM arrangements	9.1.2 Evaluation of continuity procedures	
		9.1 Monitoring, measurement, analysis and evaluation
5.1 Internal audit	9.2 Internal audit	
5.2 Management review of the BCMS	9.3 Management review	
6.1 Preventive and corrective actions	10.1 Nonconformity and corrective action 9.1.1 General	
6.2 Continual improvement	10.2 Continual improvement	

Appendix C   Interested parties' template

Interested party	Expectations of interested parties		Ranking (high/med/low)
	Under normal circumstances	During a disruption	

Date of assessment   Signed off by

....

Date to be reviewed

....

Appendix D   Sample scoping document

ACME ORGANIZATION LTD
BUSINESS CONTINUITY MANAGEMENT SCOPE

This document sets out the scope of the business continuity management system (BCMS) that is currently operated by Acme Organization Ltd.

The BCMS covers the key services of the Home Service and Commercial Contracts divisions of the organization.

The key services are:

- emergency call-out; and
- fault reporting and repair.

These services are delivered from the four regional depots based in London, Birmingham, Manchester and Glasgow.

The BCMS extends to cover all activities, resources and dependencies utilized by these key services.

The Acme Organization Ltd BCMS has been aligned to the International Organization for Standardization's ISO 22301:2012, *Societal security – Business continuity management systems – Requirements* standard.

This scoping document was issued on 1 May 2012 and will be reviewed not later than 1 May 2013.

Signed on behalf of Acme Organization Ltd

.... Dated: 1 May 2012

A B Jones, Managing Director
Acme Organization Ltd
Acme Business Park,
West Acton
London

Appendix E   Sample business continuity policy

ACME ORGANIZATION LTD

BUSINESS CONTINUITY POLICY

Introduction

The Acme Organization's business continuity policy provides the framework within which our company can comply with the business continuity requirements of our customers by introducing a business continuity management system (BCMS) that aligns with ISO 22301:2012. Business continuity management is being established to ensure our company can continue to deliver a minimum level of service to our key customers in the event of any disruption. Plans must be made, published and tested for key services as agreed by the Business Continuity Committee.

Application

The policy applies to those divisions and areas of our company set out in the scoping document. All employees within these divisions and areas must be aware of this policy. This policy applies in particular to heads of divisions and business unit managers.

Purpose

The Acme Organization's business continuity policy provides a structure through which:

- a comprehensive BCMS is established and maintained;
- key services, together with their critical processes and activities, and supporting resources and interdependencies, will be identified;
- business impact analysis and risk assessment will be applied to our critical processes and activities, supporting resources and interdependencies;

- plans will be developed to ensure continuity of key services at a minimum acceptable level and within specific timeframes following disruption;
- invocation of business continuity plans and communications with our customers and clients can be managed;
- plans are subject to ongoing exercising and revision; and
- the executive board can be assured that the BCMS remains up to date and relevant.

Policy statement

- Each key service within our company is to be owned by a designated division. The head of division will ensure that plans capable of maintaining a minimum acceptable standard of service delivery are in place for each key service.
- Functional departments will provide professional support to improve resilience of critical activities and resources that support key services.
- Each division will carry out an annual review of its business continuity process. The Business Continuity Committee will monitor the review process, benchmark the results and provide support where necessary.
- Each division must exercise its business continuity plans at least once a year and make modifications where necessary, to take account of the exercise results.
- Contracts with suppliers of critical goods and services to our company must include a requirement for the supplier's business continuity processes to be approved and to be exercised to the satisfaction of our company.
- All staff must be made aware of the plans that affect their division or business unit and their role following invocation of business continuity plans.
- Our key customers are to be kept informed about our BCM arrangements as they affect the service provided to them.

Benefits

The policy provides a clear commitment to establishing a business continuity management system within Acme Organization that will enable our company to:

- continue to provide key services to our customers in times of disruption;
- make best use of personnel and other resources at times when both may be scarce;
- reduce the period of disruption to our organization and the customers we serve;

- resume normal working more efficiently and effectively after a period of disruption;
- comply with standards of corporate governance;
- improve the resilience of our organization's infrastructure to reduce the likelihood of disruption; and
- reduce the operational and financial impact of any disruption.

Responsibilities

- The Head of Finance is responsible to the executive board for business continuity issues.
- This policy is owned by the Business Continuity Committee.
- The Head of Business Continuity within the Finance Division is the professional lead for business continuity within our company and will:
  - review and develop the policy in line with industry best practice and the needs of our company;
  - monitor the performance of the BCMS and compliance with the policy; and
  - provide support and guidance to divisional managers.

Policy review date

This policy will be subject to review by 30 April 2013.

For further enquiries please contact Head of BCM on extension 5143.

Signed on behalf of Acme Organization Ltd, Acme Business Park, West Acton, London

.... Dated: 1 May 2012

A B Jones, Managing Director

Acme Organization business continuity policy, Version 1 April 2012

Appendix F BCM competencies

The BCM team should demonstrate the ability to apply knowledge and skills in the areas listed below.

Initiation of BCMS

- Understand the principles of management systems and the Plan-Do-Check-Act approach.
- Understand the requirements of appropriate BCM standards.
- Understand the organization and its environment.
- Establish the needs and expectations of interested parties.
- Identify applicable laws, regulations and obligations.
- Establish the scope of the BCMS.
- Understand the risks to establishing, implementing and maintaining the BCMS.
- Develop and co-ordinate action plans to establish, implement and maintain the BCMS.
- Report to senior management and obtain senior management approval/commitment to BCM and the BCMS.
- Establish a BCMS structure, taking into account: roles and responsibilities, budget and resource requirements.
- Identify the competences required for those involved with the BCMS and business continuity procedures and develop appropriate training programmes.
- Develop and deliver awareness programmes.
- Establish document management and control.

Operational planning and control

- Understand BIA methodologies.
- Understand assessment techniques: quantitative and qualitative methods.
- Assess effects of disruptions, loss exposure and business impact.
- Define criticality of business functions and processes, and prioritize recovery.
- Determine recovery timeframes and minimum resource requirements.
- Understand the organization's risk appetite.
- Evaluate, select and use appropriate risk analysis methodologies and tools.
- Identify controls and safeguards to prevent and/or mitigate the effects of risk.

- Evaluate the effectiveness of controls and safeguards.

Developing BCM strategies

- Identify enterprise-wide and business unit continuity strategic requirements.
- Assess suitability of alternative strategies and select appropriate solutions.
- Identify resources required to achieve continuity strategies.
- Develop communication strategies covering all interested parties.
- Prepare a cost–benefit analysis of continuity strategies and present findings to senior management.
- Understand contractual agreements for business continuity services.

Incident response and operations

- Identify components of IRS.
- Identify incident response, business continuity and recovery team(s) and define roles and responsibilities.
- Develop detailed incident response procedures.
- Identify command and control requirements and procedures.
- Establish command centres.
- Identify applicable laws and regulations governing emergency management. Identify emergency response and triage requirements and procedures.
- Identify and co-ordinate with agencies supporting business continuity needs and aims. Identify salvage and restoration requirements.

Developing and implementing incident plans and BCM plans

- Determine plan development requirements.
- Identify and define the format and structure of major plan components.
- Draft and implement plans.

Incident communication

- Identify and develop a proactive incident communication programme.
- Establish a community-wide warning and informing system as appropriate.
- Establish essential incident communication plans with external agencies as appropriate.
- Establish essential communication plans with internal and external interested parties to ensure they are kept informed in an appropriate manner.
- Establish essential communication plans with the media.

Exercising plans

- Establish an exercise programme.
- Determine exercise requirements.
- Develop realistic scenarios.
- Establish exercise evaluation criteria and document findings.
- Develop exercises for incident communication plans.
- Develop and facilitate appropriate exercises with external agencies.
- Facilitate exercises.
- Manage post-exercise reporting.
- Monitor actions resulting from exercises and feed back to appropriate people.

Performance evaluation

- Develop appropriate evaluation metrics for BCMS and business continuity arrangements.
- Establish status-reporting procedures.
- Monitor performance of BCMS and business continuity against metrics.
- Define plan maintenance scheme and schedule.
- Undertake self-assessment of BCMS and business continuity arrangements.
- Determine audit objectives.
- Provide input to management reviews.
- Monitor actions resulting from self-assessments, audits and management reviews. Ensure resulting actions completed.

Improvement

- Identify nonconformities and initiate corrective actions.
- Establish a culture of continual improvement.

Appendix G   Establishing a training programme

People need training to equip them with the relevant knowledge and skills, and to build relationships with other team players. Key questions to be asked in developing a training programme are listed below.

Who needs to be trained?

- The BCM team.
- People named specifically in business continuity plans.
- Senior management.
- 'Non-essential' staff who may be needed at the time of plan invocation.
- Contractors and suppliers.

How are training needs identified?

For every individual/group involved in delivering the BCMS (including those involved in plan invocation) the following should be listed.

What do they need to know?

- Specific knowledge about the role.
- General understanding of what others do.
- Processes used.

What additional skills do they need?

- Specialist equipment skills.
- Interpersonal skills.

When answers have been obtained to the above questions, a training programme should be developed.

Satisfying training needs

For every individual/group involved in delivering the BCMS (including those involved in plan invocation) it is important to identify any deficiencies in skills and knowledge in relation to those required to deliver the BCMS or invoke plans. This is sometimes called a gap analysis. When deficiencies have been identified, an appropriate training programme needs to be developed to bridge the gap.

Training delivery

The training may use external or internal resources and should:

- develop skills through tutored practice as well as a self-development programme, possibly e-based;
- increase knowledge through discussion seminars and walk-through activities;
- build relationships by training with the team and through exercises.

Figure 24 sets out a possible model for developing a training programme.

Effective training and validation requires a policy and commitment from the organization, as well as the necessary resources. The training should be based on standards and targets and should also be subject to an assessment process.

It is essential to maintain a log of training for every identified individual or group involved in the BCMS.

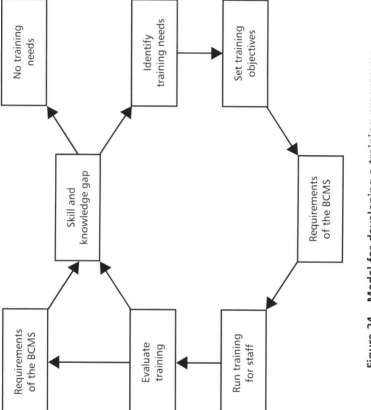

Figure 24 – Model for developing a training programme

The boxes in the figure read:

- No training needs
- Identify training needs
- Set training objectives
- Skill and knowledge gap
- Requirements of the BCMS
- Requirements of the BCMS
- Evaluate training
- Run training for staff

Appendix H   Business impact assessment matrix

Level of impact	Insignificant (1)	Minor (2)	Moderate (3)	Major (4)	Catastrophic (5)
Category					
Personal injury to customer/ staff/visitor/ contractor (A)	Minor incident. First aid administered.	Incident requiring medical treatment. Less than three-day absence. Emotional distress.	Hospital admission. More than three-day absence. Semi-permanent injury/emotional trauma.	Fatality. Permanent disability/emotional injury.	Multiple fatalities. Multiple permanent disabilities/ emotional injuries.

Level of impact		Insignificant (1)	Minor (2)	Moderate (3)	Major (4)	Catastrophic (5)
Category						
System failure (B)		Negligible service disruption. No impact on client/customer service. Minimal disruption to routine organization activity. No long-term consequences.	Single failure to meet internal service-level agreements. No impact on client/customer service. Impact on organization rapidly absorbed. No long-term consequences.	Repeated failures to meet service-level agreements. Minimal impact on client/customer service. Impact on organization absorbed with significant level of intervention. Minimal long-term consequences.	1 to 2 days' outage. Significant impact on client/customer service. Impact on organization absorbed with some formal intervention by other organizations. Significant long-term consequences.	Complete loss of systems and loss of data. Major impact on client/customer service. Impact on organization absorbed with significant formal intervention by other organizations. Major long-term consequences.

Level of impact / Category	Insignificant (1)	Minor (2)	Moderate (3)	Major (4)	Catastrophic (5)
Public confidence and reputation (C)	Issue of no public/political concern.	Local press interest. Local public/political concern.	Limited damage to reputation. Extended local press interest/regional press interest. Regional public/political concern.	Loss of credibility and confidence in organization. National press interest. Independent external inquiry. Significant public/political concern.	Prolonged national media coverage. Major public/political concern. Full public inquiry.
Failure to meet laws and regulations (D)	Legal challenge. Minor out-of-court settlement.	Civil action – no defence. Improvement notice.	Class action. Criminal prosecution. Prohibition notice.	Criminal prosecution – no defence. Executive officer dismissed.	Criminal prosecution – no defence. Executive officer fined or imprisoned.
Financial loss (E)	Less than £5,000.	£5,000–£50,000.	£50,000–£250,000.	£250,000–£1 million.	More than £1 million.

Appendix I   BIA template

BIA record for Acme Organization Ltd

	Key services/products	Areas of impact (A–E see below)	Impact (1–5)	Maximum tolerable period of disruption (MTPD)	Recovery time objective (RTO)	Minimum service level [minimum business continuity objective (MBCO)]
1						
2						
3						
4						
5						
6						
7						
8						
9						
10						

A Effect on personnel safety
B System failure
C Public confidence and reputation
D Failure to comply with legal and regulatory requirements

E Financial loss	Signed off by
Date of assessment .... Date to be reviewed	....

Appendix J   Sample resource record

Resource record for Acme Organization Ltd

Process/activity	People	Skills	Computing equipment	Software applications	Telecommunications	Information/data	Non-ICT equipment	Accommodation	Furniture	Internal dependencies	Suppliers/partners

Date of assessment

....

Date to be reviewed

....

Signed off by

....

Appendix K   Sample risk mitigation record

Risk mitigation measures for Acme Organization Ltd

Division/dept.		Key product/service		
Critical activity/resource/dependency	Risk	Ranking (H/M/L)	Risk mitigation measures	
Date of assessment		Signed off by	Date to be reviewed	

Appendix L   Resource requirements template

	Key service/product		
Division/dept.	**Key service/product**		
	Resource required		
	0–24 hours*	**Within 3 days***	**Within 14 days***
Activities that support key service/product			
People and skills required			
Computing and telecoms required			
Software applications required			
Information required			
Non-ICT equipment required			
Accommodation required			
Furniture required			
Key suppliers/partners			
Other dependencies			
Other comments			
Date of assessment	Signed off by		
Date to be reviewed			
* Timing set to suit organization's requirements.			

Appendix M   Key resource strategies

The key resource strategies below are taken from BS 25999-1:2006.

People

The organization should identify appropriate strategies for maintaining core skills and knowledge. This analysis should extend beyond employees to contractors and other stakeholders who possess extensive specialist skills and knowledge. Strategies to protect or provide those skills might include:

a) documentation of the way in which critical activities are performed;
b) multi-skill training of staff and contractors;
c) separation of core skills to reduce the concentration of risk (this might entail physical separation of staff with core skills or ensuring that more than one person has the requisite core skills);
d) use of third parties;
e) succession planning; and
f) knowledge retention and management.

[BS 25999-1:2006, Clause 7.3]

In setting the strategies in this area it is important to remember people will react differently during an emergency/major incident compared with how they operate normally. A useful resource covering these issues is BSI's PD 25111, *Business continuity management – Guidance on human aspects of business continuity*.

Premises

Worksite strategies can vary significantly and a range of options might be available. Different types of incident or threat might require the implementation of different or multiple worksite options. The correct strategies will in part be determined by the organization's size, sector and spread of activities, by stakeholders and by geographical base. For example, public authorities will need to maintain a frontline service delivery in their communities.

[BS 25999-1:2006 commentary on Clause 7.4 Premises]

The organization should devise a strategy for reducing the impact of the unavailability of its normal worksite(s). This may include one or more of the following:

a) alternative premises (locations) within the organization, including displacement of other activities;
b) alternative premises provided by other organizations (whether or not these are reciprocal arrangements);
c) alternative premises provided by third-party specialists [sometimes called work area recovery];
d) working from home or at remote sites;
e) other agreed suitable premises; and
f) use of an alternative workforce in an established site.

NOTE 1 If staff are to be moved to alternative premises, these premises ought to be close enough that staff are willing and able to travel there, taking into account any possible difficulties caused by the incident. However, the alternative premises ought not to be so close that they are likely to be affected by the same incident.

NOTE 2 The use of alternative premises for continuity purposes ought to be supported by a clear statement as to whether the alternative premises are for the sole use of the organization. If the alternative premises are shared with other organizations, a plan to mitigate the non-availability of these premises ought to be developed and documented.

[BS 25999-1:2006, Clause 7.4]

An alternative solution to relocating people to alternative premises is to provide them with remote access to IT via dial-up, or through the internet using a virtual private network (VPN) or similar technology.

NOTE 3 It may be appropriate to move the workload rather than the staff, e.g. a manufacturing line or a call centre's workload.

[BS 25999-1:2006, Clause 7.4]

Technology

Technology strategies will vary significantly between organizations according to the size, nature and complexity of business. Specific strategies ought to be developed to safeguard, replace or restore specialized or custom built technologies with long lead times.

The organization may need to make provision for manual operations before full technology services are recovered.

[BS 25999-1:2006 commentary on Clause 7.5.1 of Clause 7.5 Technology]

7.5.1 Technology strategies will depend on the nature of the technology employed and its relationship to critical activities, but will typically be one or a combination of the following:

- provision made within the organization;
- services delivered to the organization; and
- services provided externally by a third party.

7.5.2 Technology strategies may include:

- geographical spread of technology, i.e. maintaining the same technology at different locations that will not be affected by the same business disruption;
- holding older equipment as emergency replacement or spares; and
- additional risk mitigation for unique or long lead time equipment.

7.5.3 Information and communications technologies (ICT) services frequently need complex continuity strategies. Where such strategies are required, consideration should be given to:

- recovery time objectives (RTOs) for systems and applications which support the key activities identified in the BIA. [It is important that the business drives the ICT RTOs; it is possible that ICT RTOs need to be set within the RTOs specified by the business in order to facilitate testing, etc.];
- location and distance between technology sites;
- number of technology sites;
- remote access;
- the use of un-staffed (dark) sites as opposed to staffed sites;
- telecoms connectivity and redundant routing;
- the nature of "failover" (whether manual intervention is required to activate alternative IT provision or whether this needs to occur automatically); and
- third-party connectivity and external links....

[BS 25999-1:2006, Clause 7.5]

Information

Information strategies should be such as to ensure that information vital to the organization's operation is protected and recoverable according to the timeframes described within the BIA....

Any information required for enabling the delivery of the organization's critical activities should have appropriate:

- confidentiality;
- integrity;
- availability; and
- currency.

Information strategies should be documented for the recovery of information that has not yet been copied or backed-up to a safe location.

Information strategies should extend to include:

- physical (hardcopy) formats; and
- virtual (electronic) formats, etc.

NOTE 2 In all cases, information needs to be recovered to a point in time that is known and agreed by top management. Various methods of copying may be used, such as electronic or tape backups, microfiche, photocopies, creating dual copies at the time of production and so on. This known recovery point is often referred to as the "recovery point objective" [RPO].

[BS 25999-1:2006, Clause 7.6]

Supplies

In office-based environments, supplies might constitute cheques, etc. Other industries might identify retail stock or just-in-time supplies, or vehicle fuels.

[BS 25999-1:2006 commentary on Clause 7.7 Supplies]

7.7.1 The organization should identify and maintain an inventory of the core supplies that support its critical activities. Strategies to provide these may include:

- storage of additional supplies at another location;

- arrangements with third parties for delivery of stock at short notice;
- diversion of just-in-time deliveries to other locations;
- holding of materials at warehouses or shipping sites;
- transfer of sub-assembly operations to an alternative location which has supplies; and
- identification of alternative/substitute supplies.

7.7.2 Where critical activities are dependent upon specialist supplies, the organization should identify the key suppliers and single sources of supply. Strategies to manage continuity of supply may include:

- increasing the number of suppliers;
- encouraging or requiring suppliers to have a validated business continuity capability;
- contractual and/or service level agreements with key suppliers; or
- the identification of alternative, capable suppliers.

[BS 25999-1:2006, Clause 7.7]

PD 25222 published by BSI provides detailed advice on how to ensure supply chain continuity.

Appendix N Sample plan review

Business Continuity Assurance Certificate

Name of department: ....

Within my department I can confirm that the following apply:	Yes	No	If your answer to any question is 'nc' please provide information
1.	There is a high-level business continuity plan in place for my department.		
2.	The high-level business continuity plan has been sent to the departmental business continuity team for validation.		
3.	Each business area within my department has a business continuity plan in place.		
4.	Key business risks have been identified within my department and appropriate contingencies have been put in place to mitigate risks.		

Name of department: ....

Within my department I can confirm that the following apply:	Yes	No	If your answer to any question is 'no' please provide information
5.	All business continuity plans in my department conform to the standard specified by the corporate business continuity system.			
6.	All business continuity plans within my department are exercised and reviewed on a regular basis.			
7.	Business continuity roles and responsibilities within my department are clearly defined and understood.			

The business continuity plans listed below were validated by:

....[Name of department]

to support the business continuity validation and assurance process. We hold a completed business continuity validation form for each business unit that we selected for validation in this exercise. These are listed below.

No.	Name of business unit	Location	Further comments
1			
2			
3			
4			
5			
6			
7			
8			
9			
10			

Total number of business continuity plans validated:	Percentage total of departmental business continuity plans validated: ....
I confirm that this is a true and accurate picture of the current status of business continuity: **for the period 1 April** ....(insert year) **to 31 March** ....(insert year)	
Signature:	Date:
Print name:	
Position:	
Note: if you cannot provide full assurance for your department, complete the box below.	
It may be that currently you are only able to provide partial assurance with regards to business continuity arrangements within your department. If this is the case, please provide details in the box below of what action is being taken by the department to address those areas where currently you cannot provide full assurance.	

Appendix O   Sample incident log

Acme Organization Ltd				
Incident		Location		Lead manager ....
Impacted service/product				
Date and time	Information/request	From	Action taken	By whom
Signature			Date	

Appendix P   Sample business continuity plan

Acme Organization Ltd – Home Service Midlands Department

Document name	Business continuity plan – emergency call-out service
Version	V1:1, 18 May 2012
Version comment	Minor amendments following staff input, 15 May 2012
Date version	18 May 2012
Author	P. Jones, Assistant Service Manager

Plan overview including ownership

Business continuity plan – emergency call-out service

The aim of the plan is to enable the emergency call-out service of the Home Service Midlands Department of the Home Services Division to be resumed following an incident that disrupts the service. The emergency call-out service is a key service for the company as this is a contracted service to the local housing associations.

Within two hours of a disruption the company must be able to receive and respond to emergency call-out requests from housing association tenants.

This plan assumes that the public telephone service has not been affected by the disruption.

This plan is owned by the Head of the Maintenance Department of the Home Services Division.

Plan distribution

Copies of this plan are held by:

Head of the Maintenance Department, Service Manager, Home Services Division's HQ

Roles and responsibilities

The Business Unit Manager, or their deputy, is responsible for assessing the effects of a disruption and the impact on the capability of the unit to deliver the key service. If appropriate, the Business Unit Manager, or their deputy, will activate this plan in order to restore the service to the agreed service level and within the agreed timescale. The Business Unit Manager, or their deputy, will assemble their BCM team to implement the plan.

BCM Team members:

Position	Contact	Deputy	Contact
Department BCM Co-ordinator: Deputy Department BCM Co-ordinator:			
Acme Organization BCM Manager: Acme Organization Deputy BCM Manager:			

Notifications, activation and escalation rules

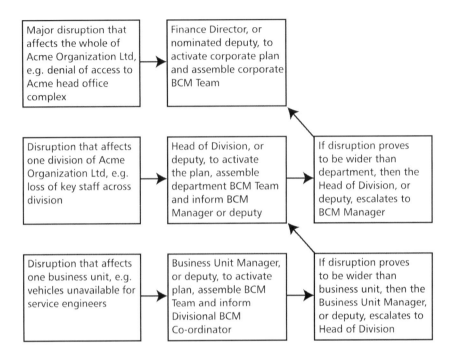

Command centre details

If required, the BCM team will assemble in the second-floor meeting room of the Midlands office. If this location is not available, the alternative location for the command centre is the welfare room at the vehicle garage on Oxleys Road.

Contact details of command centres:

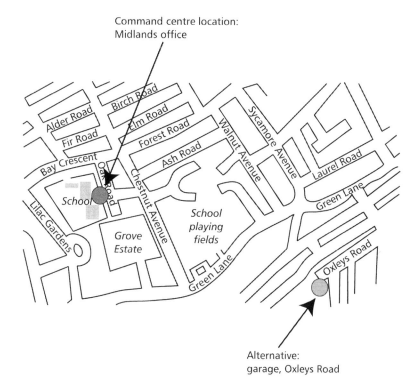

Command centre location:
Midlands office

Alternative:
garage, Oxleys Road

Facilities at command centres: telephone, internet access and battle box.

Battle box contains:..

Contacts, internal and external

Details for contacts to cover those who are:

- internal;
- external; and
- subject experts.

Task checklists

•	Mandatory tasks:	....
•	Discretionary tasks:	....

Task completion tracking process: record all actions taken, together with times, on the action/task worksheet.

Critical activities recovery plans

- Schedule of critical activities including recovery times and levels.
- Recovery plans for critical activities.
- Recovery site location(s).

Example

Minimum of two maintenance engineers to be available within two hours, operating from home if unable to operate out of normal office location or recovery location.

In the event of no staff being available, then mutual aid arrangements are in place with Any Job Anywhere Any Time Company. Contact details are listed above.

Mutual aid plan is as follows:...

Recovery resource requirements

Recovery resource requirements are:

- people;
- information/data;
- IT;
- telecommunications;
- vehicles;
- specialist equipment;
- accommodation;
- office equipment;
- furniture;
- stationery, etc.

The following supporting information not included in the plan is located as shown

• Personnel records • Handling injuries and fatalities • Staff welfare and counselling • Health and safety	{ – HR Department { { { {
• Computer equipment • Telecommunications	{ – Corporate ICT Department {
• Communicating with staff • Handling the media and PR	{ – Corporate Communications {
• Emergency services liaison	{ – Building Management
• Finance • Insurance policies • Legal advice	{ – Corporate Finance Department { {
• Communicating with suppliers and intermediaries • Supplier agreements	{ – Purchasing Department { {

Form templates

• Meetings agenda
• Decision and action log
• Task list status report
• Telephone log

Plan signed off by:

....[Head of Home Services Division]

Date to be reviewed: ....

Appendix Q Types and methods of exercising BCM arrangements

Complexity	Exercise	Process	Variants	Good practice frequency
Simple	Desk check.	Review/amendment of content.	Update/validation.	At least annually.
		Challenge content of BCP.	Audit/verification.	Annually.
Medium	Walk-through of plan.	Challenge content of BCP.	Include interaction and validate participants' roles.	Annually.
	Simulation.	Use 'artificial' situation to validate that the BCP(s) contain both necessary and sufficient information to enable a successful recovery.	Incorporate associated plans.	Annually or twice yearly.
	Exercise critical activities.	Invocation in a controlled situation that does not jeopardize business-as-usual operation.	Defined operations from alternative site for a fixed time.	Annually or less.
Complex	Exercise full BCP, including incident management.	Building/campus/exclusion zone-wide exercise.		Annually or less.

Appendix R   Suggested BCM audit checklist

Rate achievement for each key issue (1 – not started, 2 – 25 per cent complete, 3 – 50 per cent complete, 4 – 75 per cent complete, 5 – completed).

Stages	Key issues	Example evidence	Rating
Context of the organization	Identification of the organization's objectives, obligations, statutory and regulatory duties, and environment in which the organization operates. Identification of the needs and expectations of the interested parties.	Analysis of needs and expectations of interested parties. Listing of obligations, and statutory and regulatory duties.	1-2-3-4-5
	Key services and products delivered by and on behalf of the organization have been identified and have been agreed by the executive board.	Documented procedures for identifying and reviewing key services and products. Executive board minutes confirming key services and products.	1-2-3-4-5

Stages	Key issues	Example evidence	Rating
Context of the organization	Determination of the organization's risk appetite and risk criteria.	Formal risk management in place with documented evidence of risk criteria and risk appetite.	1-2-3-4-5
	A BCMS is formalized through the organization's policy and procedures.	A BCM policy and scoping documents exist. The BCM policy is published internally and externally. BCM objectives, and plans to achieve them, in place.	1-2-3-4-5
Leadership	Responsibility for BCM issues is clearly defined within the organization at the corporate management level.	Named executive director accountable for BCM policy and implementation. Reports to senior management groups.	1-2-3-4-5
	BCM Manager(s) or Co-ordinator(s) appointed.	Named individual(s) in post responsible for implementing and maintaining the BCM programme. Competence requirements documented. Training programme to establish and maintain BCM competence.	1-2-3-4-5

Stages	Key issues	Example evidence	Rating
Leadership	Responsibility for business continuity issues is well embedded within individual services or management units.	BCM is included in job descriptions and skill sets of service and support managers. BCM responsibilities enforced by inclusion in organization's appraisal, reward and recognition policies.	1–2–3–4–5
	Awareness of business continuity issues is well embedded within the organization.	There is a programme in place raising awareness throughout the organization and its interested parties. Feedback mechanisms exist whereby functional managers and staff can flag up BCM issues. Evidenced through minutes of meetings and reports. Induction programmes include awareness of BCM.	1–2–3–4–5

Stages	Key issues	Example evidence	Rating
Operational planning and control	Critical processes, activities, and supporting resources and dependencies, within and without the organization, that are needed to deliver the key services and products, have been identified.	Documentation detailing critical processes, activities, and supporting resources and dependencies. Mapping of critical suppliers and partners.	1–2–3–4–5
	Identification of the impact, over time, on the organization and the interested parties of the loss of any key service or product.	A structured business impact analysis (BIA) process exists for the organization that prioritizes key services and products. A documented BIA that covers the key services and products of the organization. Executive board minutes confirming BIA.	1–2–3–4–5
	Risk assessment has been used on the critical activities, and supporting resources and dependencies, to focus effort on the areas of greatest need.	Documented procedures to review and rank risk. Identification of 'single points of failure'.	1–2–3–4–5
	Countermeasures exist to minimize risks that have been identified, including measures to combat potential loss of information.	Documented evidence of risk mitigation covering people, systems, information, premises and equipment, and suppliers.	1–2–3–4–5

Stages	Key issues	Example evidence	Rating
Determining business continuity strategies	Development of appropriate strategies to limit, over time, the impact of the loss of key services and products on the organization and interested parties.	Documented strategies to support each key service and product. Strategies cover: people, premises, technology, information, supplies and communications with interested parties. Strategies take account of public authority's actions, including those undertaken in an emergency situation. Executive board minutes confirming strategy selection and its required resource allocations.	1–2–3–4–5
	Development of strategies to minimize supplier disruption.	Procurement policies for key suppliers that require BCM to be incorporated into their supply contracts. Evidence of BCM included in supply contracts. Suppliers' BCM arrangements audited. Alternative suppliers identified.	1–2–3–4–5

Stages	Key issues	Example evidence	Rating
Establishing and implementing BCM procedures	Incident response structure in place. Incident management plans are developed. Generic business continuity plans (BCPs) are developed that are flexible enough to maintain continuity of key services and products through a range of disruptive events.	Details of incident response structure and procedures. Structure and procedures for developing incident management and business continuity plans. Reports. Meeting minutes. Plans are clear, unambiguous and easy to use. Documented evidence of consultation with relevant staff in functional units and incorporation of feedback during plan development. Plans identify objectives, personnel involved, and command and control arrangements. Plans contain references to other sources of relevant information, advice and other documentation.	1–2–3–4–5
	A clear procedure exists for invoking the plans and delivering the response.	Documented invocation and response procedures. Key staff are identified in plans. Call-out lists for incident and continuity team members.	1–2–3–4–5
	Plans have clear ownership and are signed off at the appropriate level.	It is clear who is responsible for ensuring that each section/department or site has plans. All plans are signed off by plan owners and/or nominated managers.	1–2–3–4–5

Stages	Key issues	Example evidence	Rating
Establishing and implementing BCM procedures	Appointment of teams that are trained to deliver the plans.	Details of incident and continuity team members. Competence assessment undertaken. Training programme for team members. Training record for team members.	1–2–3–4–5
	A clear procedure exists that ensures interested parties, internal and external, are aware of what actions the organization will take if plans are activated.	A communications policy document. Letters, emails, circulars, meeting minutes, and internet and intranet pages that raise awareness of the plans.	1–2–3–4–5
	Ensuring communications with interested parties at the time of disruption to key services and products.	Plans containing arrangements for communicating with clients, customers, staff, partners, interested parties and the media. Plans linked to communications plans.	1–2–3–4–5

Stages	Key issues	Example evidence	Rating
Establishing and implementing BCM procedures	Ensuring latest plans and supporting materials are always available.	Copies of plans and essential equipment/documents (in electronic or hard copy) are easily available on and off site. All plans are subject to document and version control processes.	1–2–3–4–5
	Plans linked to other event plans within and without the organization.	Links to emergency, recovery, major incident, information and communications technology disaster recovery (ICT DR), and communications plans, etc. are documented.	1–2–3–4–5
	Documented procedures to recover business activities post incident.	Appropriate recovery plans and procedures in place.	1–2–3–4–5

Stages	Key issues	Example evidence	Rating
Exercising	Ensuring there is a balanced programme of exercise types that validates the full range of BCM capabilities.	Records of regularly tested contact arrangements and exercises. Exercise programmes/test schedules.	1–2–3–4–5
	Exercise programmes have clear objectives.	Exercise scenarios and plans.	1–2–3–4–5
	Ensuring there is a documented process for capturing and taking forward the lessons identified from exercises and tests.	Notes of exercise debriefs and 'lessons identified' reports. Exercise review reports to relevant management team. Action plans. Review of actions at plan preparation/review meetings. Evidence that the lessons learnt from exercises have been incorporated into plans.	1–2–3–4–5

Stages	Key issues	Example evidence	Rating
Performance evaluation	Assurance of organization's BCM capability.	Key performance indicators (KPIs) set for BCM implementation and maintenance. KPIs subject to regular review. BCM responsibilities reviewed by the organization's audit process.	1–2–3–4–5
	A clear mechanism is in place for measuring the effectiveness of the BCMS.	BCMS review programme. Self-assessment reports. Internal audit reports. Benchmarking against standards (e.g. ISO 22301) and guidelines. External reviews by peers from other organizations.	1–2–3–4–5
	Ensuring that the plans are kept up to date.	There is an established and documented plan review process. Plan review is built into the business planning cycle. Plan reviews are up to date and signed by nominated manager. Notes from review meetings. Issue of version-controlled updates and acknowledgement system for recipients.	1–2–3–4–5

Stages	Key issues	Example evidence	Rating
Performance evaluation	Ensuring there is a documented process for capturing and taking forward the lessons identified from incidents or near misses.	Notes of incident debriefs, lessons identified, action reports and results.	1–2–3–4–5
	Ensuring that when there are major changes to the organization or the environment in which it operates, or threats, the BCM programme is reviewed and modified as appropriate.	There is a mechanism that triggers BCM reviews. Action plans. Review of actions at plan preparation/review meetings. Notes from review meetings.	1–2–3–4–5
	Ensuring that the review process drives improvement by identifying lessons, and appropriate action is taken.	Review reports to relevant management team. Action plans. Review of actions at BCMS review meetings. Evidence that the lessons learnt from reviews have been incorporated into the organization's BCMS.	1–2–3–4–5
Improvement	Nonconformities with the BCMS are identified and corrective actions taken as appropriate.	There is a formalized process for identifying and correcting nonconformities in the organization's BCMS. Notes from management review meetings.	1–2–3–4–5

References

Airmic (2011) *Roads to Ruin – A Study of Major Risk Events: Their Origins, Impact and Implications*, a report by Cass Business School on behalf of Airmic, London: Airmic

ASIS/BSI BCM.01-2010, *Business Continuity Management Systems: Requirements with Guidance for Use*, New York: American National Standards Institute

British Insurance Brokers' Association (BIBA) and UK Cabinet Office (2012), *The Value of Business Continuity Planning*, London: British Insurance Broker's Association

BS 25999-1:2006, *Business continuity management — Part 1: Code of practice*, London: British Standards Institution

BS 25999-2:2007, *Business continuity management — Part 2: Specification*, London: British Standards Institution

BS EN ISO 9001:2008, *Quality management systems — Requirements*, London: British Standards Institution

BS EN ISO 14001:2004, *Environmental management systems — Requirements with guidance for use*, London: British Standards Institution

Chartered Management Institute (2012) *Planning for the worst. The 2012 Business Continuity Management Survey (March 2012)*, London: Chartered Management Institute

Great Britain (2004) *Civil Contingencies Act 2004*, London: The Stationery Office

HM Government (2005) *Emergency Preparedness, Guidance on Part 1 of the Civil Contingencies Act 2004, its associated Regulations and non-statutory arrangements*, London: UK Cabinet Office

ISO 22301:2012, *Societal security – Business continuity management systems – Requirements,* Geneva: International Organization for Standardization

ISO/DIS 22313, *Societal security – Business continuity management systems – Guidance,* Geneva: International Organization for Standardization. (Expected to be published during the latter part of 2012 or early 2013.)

Knight, R F and Pretty, D J (2000) *The Impact of Catastrophes on Shareholder Value,* The Oxford Executive Research Briefings, Templeton College, University of Oxford

Nassim Nicholas Taleb (2007) *The Black Swan: The Impact of the Highly Improbable,* New York: Random House

Novartis International AG (2011) *Our Code of Conduct,* Basel, Switzerland: Novartis International AG

PAS 56:2003, *Guide to business continuity management,* London: British Standards Institution (PAS 56:2003 is now withdrawn. Please see BS 25999-1:2006.)

PD 25111:2010, *Business continuity management – Guidance on human aspects of business continuity,* London: British Standards Institution

PD 25222:2011, *Business continuity management – Guidance on supply chain continuity,* London: British Standards Institution

PD 25666:2010, *Business continuity management – Guidance on exercising and testing for continuity and contingency programmes,* London: British Standards Institution

PD 25888:2011, *Business continuity management – Guidance on organization recovery following disruptive incidents,* London: British Standards Institution

Porter, E M (1985) *Competitive Advantage: Creating and Sustaining Superior Performance,* New York: Simon & Schuster

Turnbull, N et al. (1999) *Internal Control — Guidance for Directors on the Combined Code,* London: Institute of Chartered Accountants in England and Wales.

More Business Continuity Insight from BSI

Business Continuity Management for Small and Medium Sized Enterprises – How to Survive a Major Disaster or Failure
David Lacey

Don't think you have the resource to implement a business continuity system, or can't see the business justification? Then this is the book to get you started. Simple, tried and tested approaches are set out to enable businesses of any size and with a minimum of budget, time and staff to put in place effective continuity solutions that will help keep customers happy during and after a disruption.

Read more and download a free chapter: http://shop.bsigroup.com/bip2217

A Practical Approach to Business Impact Analysis – Understanding the Organization through Business Continuity Management
Ian Charters

An effective business impact analysis (BIA) is vital to the success of any continuity plan. But what is it, and how do you do it? This book clearly explains the concept and benefits, then goes on to deliver a simple and practical method for conducting a BIA that meets the particular needs of your business.

Read more and download a free chapter: http://shop.bsigroup.com/bip2214

Auditing Business Continuity Management Plans – Assess and Improve Your Performance Against ISO 22301
John Silltow

Why audit your BCM plans? One reason is that ISO 22301 requires an internal audit of the business continuity management system to be undertaken by all organizations. Another is that it provides independent assurance that the system is adequate and properly managed. This book delivers the in-depth information and knowledge needed by auditors to advise effectively on each part of the business continuity process.

Read more and download a free chapter: http://shop.bsigroup.com/bip2151

Business Continuity Communications – Successful Incident Communication Planning with ISO 22301
Jim Preen

More than ever before, communication during a disruption is a major factor in your business' ability to emerge strongly on the other side. The bad news is that it is easy to get it wrong. The good news is that preparation is everything. Packed with practical examples, inside tips, checklists and templates, this book provides all of the tools needed to feel confident when communicating in a crisis, whatever the audience.

Read more and download a free chapter: http://shop.bsigroup.com/bip2185

Business Continuity Exercises and Tests – Delivering Successful Exercise Programmes with ISO 22301
edited by Jim Preen

How can you be sure that your business continuity plans will actually work if called in to action? By testing them. This practical book will help you to decide what type of exercises and tests are appropriate to your business and its likely risks, and gives thorough, step-by-step guidance on carrying them out effectively. Case studies and scenarios are provided to make running your own exercises easier, as well as templates for recording and evaluating performance.

Read more and download a free chapter: http://shop.bsigroup.com/bip2143